THE WOMAN'S VOICE

T0347880

Winifred Edith (Nanna) and Margaret Edna (Mother).
Morecambe, 1944.

THE WOMAN'S VOICE

PATSY RODENBURG

methuen | drama

LONDON • NEW YORK • OXFORD • NEW DELHI • SYDNEY

METHUEN DRAMA
Bloomsbury Publishing Plc
50 Bedford Square, London, WC1B 3DP, UK
1385 Broadway, New York, NY 10018, USA
29 Earlsfort Terrace, Dublin 2, Ireland

BLOOMSBURY, METHUEN DRAMA and the Methuen Drama logo are
trademarks of Bloomsbury Publishing Plc

First published in Great Britain 2023

Cover design: Ben Anslow

A catalogue record for this book is available from the British Library.

A catalog record for this book is available from the Library of Congress.

ISBN: HB: 978-1-3502-7655-0
      PB: 978-1-3502-7654-3
      ePDF: 978-1-3502-7657-4
      eBook: 978-1-3502-7656-7

Typeset by RefineCatch Limited, Bungay, Suffolk

To find out more about our authors and books visit www.bloomsbury.com
and sign up for our newsletters.

Dedicated to my dear and loyal friend **Alaknanda Samarth**; a fearless and authentic voice stubbornly seeking truth and justice; a brilliant artist and mentor. Ever grateful to have known you for so long and to have encountered your spirit, intellect and heart so often.

In memory of those who generously shared wisdom: **John Roberts**; **Ron Eyre**; **John Scarlet**; **Gwynne Thurburn**; **Cecily Berry**; **Kristin Linklater**; **Sheila Moriarty**; **Margo Braund**; **Joan Washington**; **Jill Cadell**; **Tony Sher**; **Brent Carver**.

For friends: **Martin Sherman**; **Brigid Lamour**; **Johnny Yiannakis**; **Sonny Beycher**; **Susan Leverick**; **Jane Pennyfather**; **Kelly McEvenue**; **Sue Lefton**; **Sue Barnet**; **Eliot Shrimpton**; **Dympna Cunnane**; **Jacqueline McMenamin**; **Kim Krejus**; **Ruth Padel**; **Lenny Goodings**; **Andrew** and **Zoe Law**.

For their patience in the production of the book: **Rachel Clements**, my agent; **Lacey Chu** for her story; **Amy Leavitt** for her diligence and **Sally Orson-Jones**, the most wonderful editor.

Lastly, to my dear son **Michael Franceschi**.

CONTENTS

PROLOGUE

But break my heart, for I must hold my tongue.

Hamlet

This book is the story of every woman and her voice. Our fully released power and our stories. Maya Angelou wrote about the great agony of an untold story: holding your tongue hurts.

This is also the story of a curious, stubborn, sometimes arrogant and always diligent little girl, who wanted to understand why she had difficulty speaking, and why all the magnificent women around her were disempowered, masking their bodies, breath, voice and opinions.

A girl born in 1953, eight years after the end of World War II.

A girl who would play on bomb sites with the boys, which was more fun than the doll's house with its smiling, well-dressed miniature women. A child energetically aware of the grief of the adults around her, believing that their life, married to grief, was normal.

It was a time of loss, but also a time of moving through the loss.

It is possible that no family in Europe was without personal loss. There were secrets; what had been seen or done, experienced or perpetrated. Not a time for the sharing of emotions or an unchecked, unbounded voice, but a time of carrying on and silently trying to heal.

This young girl did not meet a visionary woman fighting for equal rights; it was a world that didn't even hint at the possibility of power outside the running of the house or the caring for children. A girl who knew, without any outside instruction, that this exclusion from worldly power wasn't fair.

Me.

Patricia Anne. Named after my mother's best friend, but a name my father thought sounded like a sneeze. So it moved, before I can remember, into Patsy.

Not a particularly gifted child, but one who worked hard at understanding unfairness. A girl, and later a woman, who always found communicating difficult.

This book is about the loss, the refinding and the healing of female voices.

All the women I loved; my mother, my nanna, teachers who I could feel were gagged, who couldn't share what they wanted to share.

This is the ancient and modern proof of magnificent women's voices and stories, and the constant, but failed, crusade to silence them.

1
THE BEGINNINGS

Macbeth *What is that noise?*
Seaton *It is the cry of women.*

I was born at home in a council flat in Pimlico, London. We lived on the third floor, my mother's best friend lived on the ground floor. There was a family story that the friend could hear my cry as 'clear as a bell', deep and resonant, through all the walls and floors that separated us. No problem with my voice then . . .

Lying on my back as a baby my body is naturally aligned. The huge weight of my head is held by the floor. Shoulders supported and fully released which, with the placement of my head, means my throat is open. I can open my mouth as large as I need to release sound.

My baby body knows, without having to think, that in order to power life – and alongside that, my voice – I need breath.

The first moment of life outside the womb is an intake of breath followed by a cry, a call to the world. And with that breath the heart is fuelled for emotions, and the brain for thought.

The knowledge hidden in the word 'inspiration' is true. We need to take a full breath to catch an idea. We need to take a full breath to inspire and be inspired. And throughout life, we have to make a choice to fully breathe to face and experience feelings we do not want to face, to remember what we do not want to remember. The last moment of life is the final release of breath. The final letting go of ourselves.

I often wonder at what point my baby-self chose to not fully breathe, and to copy the breath of my parents who did not want to feel. Without thought, like most babies, I knew that breath determines the volume of the sound I needed to make.

Organically, the intake of breath opens the ribcage, front, sides and back, without any lift in the shoulders or upper chest, and as the ribs open, the diaphragm (a muscle attached around the bottom of the ribcage and one that we can't feel) moves down, flattening from a dome shape. With this movement we feel the muscles of the lower abdomen move down into the groin. The lower the breath, the more power in the body and the voice, and the more we feel alive and present.

All babies know this. The more urgent, emotional and large the sound needs to be to get attention, the deeper the breath.

This deep breath is hard to get when lying on your back. The abdominal muscles fall in with gravity, so they need help to fully and powerfully engage. If the baby is not swaddled they will lift up their legs, knees bent, feet and calves dangling. This position engages the lower breath muscles – a column of air that supports all human movement, sound, feeling and thought – and facilitates a large and potent sound.

The vocal range is free and flexible, so the baby makes the sound they need. They sound as they feel, and if they feel safe they are what they sound.

The first action of the natural breath is the intake. The second is a moment of suspension when the muscles pause. Then the rib and abdominal muscles move in to release the breath. There is another brief suspension before we breathe in again.

This mighty and powerful breath supports every part of our full presence.

When we lose this full breath, and most women do, we lose our power and authority. Any loss of breath, even a slight loss, will result in a dimming of ourselves. As we breathe in we gather our power, as we breathe out we release it into the world. Breath is so important to us, that anything that goes wrong in life beds into the breath before other parts of us begin to feel what is happening.

In 1978 I was teaching a group of doctors in North London. They had asked me to help them improve their ability to communicate with their patients. We were discussing how a natural, free voice gets locked and caged into a body. We concluded that it all starts and ends with the breath. As soon as the natural rhythm of breath has been disturbed, the voice will suffer, and will no longer be free. After the session, one of the doctors stayed behind. He was intrigued about my suspicion that all our voice problems start with the breath and he invited me to visit one of his wards.

I met him there two days later and he took me at once into a ward. A ward for babies.

'Listen,' he said.

I did.

I heard what he had heard. These babies cried with a held, strained and troubled voice, not the free call that they should have. The doctor saw my shock.

'Look at their breath patterns,' he said. I realized what he meant: I could actually see that their breath rhythm was fragmented, gasping and blocked.

'All of them have been physically abused.'

They were battered babies.

The shock was intense and visceral. I felt it lock me down. These voices had been dramatically changed so soon, so palpably, in under a year of life.

Both girls and boys were in the ward. All had suffered an appalling welcome into the world, and the abuse had swiftly entered their breath, and then their voice.

My belief, shaped by my encounter with the doctor, is that as a baby cries out they are disturbed and need a guardian to help them.

When picked up and held gently and soothed, the baby stops crying, but the trauma of the cry is not released until the baby sighs. This form of a sigh resets the natural breath, and simultaneously helps to release the trauma that caused the cry in the first place.

A loving, safe and gentle hug would help reset every human's breath at whatever age, after any trauma. My experience with the doctor also provided me with an answer to a puzzle I had been agitated about since the age of six.

When I was four we moved out of London to the suburbs. We had a garden, and by the time I was six there was a swing.

This swing was my joy, particularly as my mother taught me to jump off of it. A successful jump, she explained, was achieved when you felt the exact moment of the backward suspension as you sat on the swing, before it swung into the forward trajectory, and into the release moment that propelled you off the seat. That moment of backward suspension was the feeling you needed in order to jump successfully.

I realized that this motion was linked to my breath. My jump was good as long as I got my breath fully married to that backward suspension. The jump started at that moment. I had to start breathing out as soon as the swing moved forward and that breath carried me safely to the ground.

I spent hours on that swing. It comforted me and I knew that it did. Whenever I was upset, if I could get on the swing, I could reset my breath and myself. I recognized that my distress was displayed by me not having my breath in tune with the swing's suspension, and that if I jumped without that sensitivity I would crash and hurt myself.

The swing, then, was my replacement for a hug and being cradled. Although very loving, my mother and nanna were not huggers, and so I found another way to reset my breath when disturbed.

In due course the baby begins to walk. As they stand, it is critical that they feel the floor through their feet, particularly the front of the foot.

The feet earth us. Our full breath is reliant on the connection we feel through the earth.

Full and economic human power, physical and vocal, is reliant on two points of engagement. Our strength is not in the upper chest but in our feet and lower breath. This can be easily demonstrated if you try to push a heavy object. Strong arms and an upright spine are important, but the foundation of the strong human voice and upright body is in the feet supporting the breath from the low abdominal muscles.

The importance of the feet and lower breath cannot be overstated, and for women this is a crucial understanding as it is fashion and culture that impedes these two power points for them. Be it shoes, foot binding, holding your stomach in, tight clothing, clothing that if you move in a particular way reveals too much of your body.

Is it an accident that we are taught to look as though we cannot run or breathe with power?

Most four year olds will have a properly aligned spine when they sit.

The spine holds up the body, and if it slumps it stops the free passage of the breath, and displaces the head, which tightens the voice.

All these are physical distortions that appear more in young girls than in boys, and they are appearing sooner now than they did when I started teaching forty-five years ago. When I am in primary and secondary schools now, I see young girls standing without a stable base because their feet aren't earthed and their knees are locked. Their pelvic area is pushed forwards, resulting in shoulder and upper chest tension. These physical tensions block breath and voice, resulting in their presence and delivery being underpowered.

I rarely meet an eighteen-year-old woman without some or all of these distortions. They are rarer in young men. Some of these tensions only appeared thirty years ago. This is partly because of lifestyle, but it is also foisted on girls as a point of fashion; and all the fashion habits that are presented to them, weaken them.

I know now that from the age of four I had a vocation – a calling – to study voice, breathing and speaking. I didn't know that it was to do with anatomy or presence, but what I saw was women being ignored, left out and excluded. I didn't have the words I have now, but as I grew older I fought anyone suggesting a girl was stupid: I knew I wasn't stupid, but the powerless sense of its outrageous unfairness did embed into my voice and confidence.

I have always struggled with breathing and speaking fluently, and was constantly told I was shy or had nothing to say. But this didn't feel true. I had many thoughts and ideas and longed to speak.

I wanted to understand why I couldn't express myself freely, but more importantly I wanted to know why women, women that I loved and knew were intelligent and passionate, were being silenced. Fortunately, they had not, to my knowledge, been silenced with violence, but with a contempt for their working class lack of education and by the subtle power of men politely ignoring them.

The women in my early life were much more interesting than they sounded.

In the half-century of my personal passion around teaching the importance of stories, presence and voice, I have met clients and students who cannot understand the 'great agony' of an untold story being trapped inside you.

Without exception, those bemused by the agony of not being able to speak their story are men.

My first conscious encounter with the inequality of the stories that are freely told and those trapped, was in the early 1970s and was through a conversation I had with a teacher at The Royal Central School, where I was studying. It was with the brilliant novelist and educationalist, Audrey Laski. Audrey slowly and carefully spoke a list to me of those who are heard without much challenge:

'Privileged
White
Christian
Heterosexual
Able-bodied
Men.'

The list lit up my brain, and as the kaleidoscope does as it settles itself, produced a clear shape and pattern for me to see, feel and understand the world differently.

The importance of this list cannot be underestimated. Although some of the words are dated, it was the first, clear description I had heard defining the growing debate about 'political correctness', and it produced a clarity in me, a sudden understanding that *of course* this was what inequality was all about. That the rest of us were up against the unfair elite, the entitled men who from their first breath and cry were not only listened to, but validated.

The equality laws that were to be passed in the UK in the mid-1970s would instigate progress and begin to release the stories of the silenced groups who were not on Audrey's list.

Change takes time, and teaching has to change with the times. Every day I hear stories that give me hope, but I still wonder whether Audrey knew how accurate the order of her list was: privileged, white, Christian, heterosexual, able-bodied men. I have met men who are not privileged, non-white, non-Christian, non-heterosexual, non-able-bodied, that have found their whole voice and told their stories freely. Yes, they have struggled. Yes, they have worked. But they have eventually taken their right for granted.

I have never met a woman, even those who many would consider privileged, who has been able to do this. All of them have been punished in some way for daring to be whole and fully present in the world.

At the bottom of every heap is a woman.

The 'great agony' of not speaking or sharing a story is felt in the body. It is contained in us, and reduces our human life force: the power of the breath and presence, and, consequently, our voice. It is not imagined, but real, and our wholeness is fragmented and we feel diseased. This containment can be released, and our whole presence and voice refound: The Woman's Voice.

I knew by the age of eight that women were not allowed to have their full vocal, intellectual and spiritual power in front of men. I knew that women's emotional power, their tears and rage, were mocked or found disgusting by men, and I knew that a man did not need to listen to women; and if he did the women should feel gratitude.

I had observed how women needed to be liked and therefore were skilled in putting on masks, smiling and flattering, and then criticizing men when they left the room. I realized this was because they could not show their true feelings.

I saw men charm powerful or attractive women, but occasionally I heard them deride them when they didn't think I was listening. My father switching on the charm, switching off when my mother spoke, actively ignoring my nanna.

I observed all and more but had no one to discuss it with. My sister and friends were happy with the duplicity: I was not.

It seemed mean of my father, and somehow I found my mother's ability to settle some sort of score with him by honing barely audible mocking barbs to send his way equally upsetting.

I knew that women were trapped because they were not equal. Teachers told me, boys and men told me, and my mother lived her inequality instead of showing the world her sharp and brilliant mind.

Her life unexamined, her well-being and economic safety were entirely dependent on my father, even though when they married she was being rapidly promoted through the ranks of the civil service. She earned more than he managed for a few years afterwards.

It was his requirement that she stopped work and had no access to his money, never knew what he earned and had to ask for everything.

From the age of nine I was reluctantly sent to elocution teachers to help me speak, which was for me and the teachers an unsuccessful experience, but my formal vocation started at that point.

I met and fell in love with William Shakespeare . . . Shakespeare must be a black girl.

Maya Angelou

I met Shakespeare when I was nine. Not at school, but in a battered *Complete Works* hidden in a wardrobe in my home. A surprising find in a house with no books. What a relief it was, and still is, to read the words he gave to women. They fearlessly witnessed the tyranny of men, outwitted them, eschewed their scorn and tested their legal authority. In his plays, I found men who recognized women's emotional, intellectual and spiritual equality – and loved them for it. Often a lone man defying male contempt for women; a decent man emerging to support and love these 'unlovable' women. A man swimming against the tide of the accepted inequality of women. A champion in an unfair world.

As a child, I was constantly outraged that most productions of Shakespeare I saw played the women weak and whining, which – even then – I knew wasn't what he had written. The Shakespeare I understand and teach is a beacon of humanism and fairness, a moral visionary, who stayed present with all his characters, and wrote their flaws along with their magnificences, always with compassion and often with forgiveness. He stole stories, no doubt from women, but took the essence and structure and deepened and heightened it. Then he dared us to look at our sameness and our complexity, and then at our shadows that offend.

To be or not to be, that is the question.

This line is the opening of one of Hamlet's most famous speeches. Hamlet, a privileged man, who has only recently lost a sense of his presence, struggles to reconnect after the trauma and consequences of his father's murder. This is something that every one of us, especially women, can connect with.

In the first years of my career, I knew that the free and abandoned voice most people are born with is eroded in some and maintained in others. I could see this in their bodies and breath systems, and hear it in the constraint of their voices. I then began to realize the source of the loss: it was of their authentic presence. They were not *being*. And that *is* the question.

The see-saw

We lose our authentic presence, or being, in one of two ways.

The first and the most common and easiest choice, is to disappear from the source that seeks to silence you. You can see it in the bodies of others, or feel it in yourself. It is an energetic implosion; eyes not looking out at the world, body being pulled, squashed, warped, diminished, making it less powerful. A reduction of the breath. Holding, locking and fracturing breath rhythms. If you withdraw even temporarily around people and situations that make you fearful, you can feel this. You can feel this implosion. You will avoid making too much sound with your voice, laughing too loudly, screaming out too much, speaking your opinion or your truth, and make choices that will please the one with power over you. This might mean that you are shielded and guarded, and yet, you may be found useful, or even attractive. Therefore, this choice has a safety in it, and if you feel safe for long enough, you might be able to control the one who thinks they have the power without them knowing it.

The second choice is a hard one, and will mean at best that you are cast out from the seat of power; sent away. At worst, you risk punishment. This choice is all about bluff: being too loud, taking up too much space. Voice pushed and too insistent. A physical and vocal fight for space and attention.

The unequal rarely have the luxury of being in their true and authentic presence and in their natural embodiment of body, breath and voice. The place we all seek and somehow know exists. A place of balance. In ancient and even not too distant times in schools such as Eton, this balance was the template taught to leaders. The idea was that they would learn how to use their power, but not abuse it. The place between aggression and passive-aggression. The place the unequal were never expected to occupy.

The fulcrum of the see-saw: not up, not down, but in-between.

There has been for thousands of years a fully conscious campaign by all current major civilizations to, if not destroy, then to erode women's natural power. This campaign is physically embodied in almost every woman's presence, body and voice.

No woman has escaped, even if it is only observed in the smallest physical twitch, pullback or concession.

Women have had legal equality in the UK for nearly fifty years but most are still sitting on the down seat of the see-saw. Some have progressed to the upward seat, and a frighteningly small few have managed to find the sweet-spot of balance, in the fulcrum of their power.

These are magnificent women who have worked harder and are more talented than most men on the planet.

2
CAGES

If you bring forth what is within you, what you bring forth will save you. If you do not bring forth what is within you, what you do not bring forth will destroy you.

The Gospel of St Thomas

This defines what happens to us, body, mind, heart and spirit, when energy is trapped or released. The description of being trapped applies to most women, and many men. This is the profound journey that has been discussed by women for thousands of years, and intensely focused upon in the last fifty.

By the age of fifteen I had discovered the real enemy that had caged women's voices. A thing I loved and then hated in equal measure: Western civilization as handed to us by the Ancient Greeks.

The plays, poetry, philosophy, debate and intellectual curiosity are thrilling and I loved it, but the complete dismissal of female power, I hated. Even the most privileged women were locked up and reserved for sexual and domestic duties – without hope of freedom.

I hadn't, at fifteen, realized this was a movement that had occurred almost simultaneously around the planet, and is at the heart and in the spiritual belief systems of all major civilizations and organized faiths.

I hadn't realized that there were still communities that honoured the power and voice of women. Communities that we now call indigenous. Communities that honour nature, and are the ones who have the wisdom to conserve and heal the planet.

My contribution to the healing of women starts with the simple. It is about doing, not explaining, and it *is* simple. You have to do the simple before you can understand, let alone do, the profound. The work has to be done and delivered. It is physical, takes time, and cannot be understood through intellectual explaining. Our stories, if they are to have any impact on the world, particularly on the people who don't want to hear them, have to be audible and clear. We who are not welcome in a space cannot expect to engage unsympathetic listeners unless we fully deliver our voice and words, and are compelling.

This full delivery takes practise. Practise out loud, not trapped in your head. It's a physical commitment to your presence, voice and words. This is a craft, and craft is about embodiment and hard, repetitive, simple work. I haven't yet found a way of releasing stories or the storyteller, without simple routines. I can explain how voices and stories work in a two-hour keynote presentation, but even if I manage to make that very entertaining, no one present will have much luck in improving their presence or voice until they do the work and keep practising it.

Later in this book, I will teach you how to refind your voice and your full vocal power, and sustain it.

The craft involved in teaching presence and voice has two basic stages.

The first stage is to return the body, breath and voice to their freest and most released state. It involves a cleaning out of all the tensions the body has gathered through years of trauma. Some of this trauma is very subtle; it can be the *drip, drip, drip* of being ignored. Or, it can be a major event that has blocked our breath and voice dramatically.

Understanding is important in this process, because any challenge to our authentic presence, either ignoring it or punishing it, is traumatic – particularly in a child.

In this first stage of work, we return our presence, body and breath to their full potential and maximum power. Then, we have to consolidate this with repetition, so that our presence and voice can weather stress and fear. Like all craftspeople, we have to know the work so well that we forget it.

For some, this first process is enough. But those who want to use their voices professionally and with full effect, have to stretch and expand their presence and voice, so it can be used powerfully every day, in all situations, and remain healthy.

I was fortunate enough in my early career to work with dancers, singers, martial artists and elite athletes, and these early encounters taught me that voice work is a serious physical commitment. You have to fully use your voice on a daily basis for it to maintain its range and power.

The other revelation from working with these people who so completely inhabited their own bodies, was that embodied voice exercises can work, with small adjustments, for everyone, because they are based on our shared design.

I didn't go seeking this idea of our sameness: it was thrust at me. I am the product of a generation of women who were too shy and too fearful to put themselves forward. Early in my career, I was asked to work with people outside my experience, and in cultures and spaces I'd never imagined entering.

I never knocked on a door and asked any group to learn my tradition, but was approached because someone had noticed similarities between their work and mine. I began to understand that I wasn't teaching exercises discovered by a Victorian elocution teacher, but exercises and craft forged by the human species to tell important stories.

These exercises are not invented, but are of us.

They are part of ancient wisdom, refound and retaught for thousands of years. But in recent centuries, they have been appropriated by patriarchal societies, and taught only to privileged men. No woman has been unharmed. They have walked through a valley of inequality. Worshipped if beautiful and wealthy, but not recognized as equal.

It was the curse on all women in the UK until the Sex Discrimination Act of 1975 and the Race Relations Act of 1976. And as all curses do, it had a gift. Women were knowingly or unknowingly experts on how power works. We knew the deal and we had become skilled in strategies that men had, for centuries, believed were duplicity.

Even if you had an enlightened father, husband and male friends, you would still have to walk past the male knowledge of your legal inequality every day in the street, at school or at work. You and your power and voice were hampered, if not brutally destroyed.

Some women survived by pretending to be weak or stupid, or let their beauty be their shield to stay safe in a savage world. To be liked, to find sympathy and get their way in an unequal war. Truly, there is no blame attached to this form of survival. Easier so often to do this than to be a woman who refused these masks and who was therefore punished for being true to themselves, or outcast from their community.

There is a sameness in the important stories we tell. There is invention in how you frame and tell a story, but they all stem from common human sources and preoccupations. Love, power, justice and loss. Every one of us has at some point in their life, been kept awake at night, distressed or excited by one or all of these things. At the bottom of all great stories, the source is universal.

In 1975 I was twenty-two, and along with all feminists, was joyous at our new, legal equality.

We were combative, aggressive and expected immediate change. I was naïve and believed that men would willingly trot in harness with the law and yield to our new status. My well-rehearsed routine to men who weren't trotting happily along was, 'Men's life will be happier when we are equal, we can share power and help pull the cart.'

It was simple: *All will be well on the planet when men release their power over us.*

I actually believed that after thousands of years, men would concede 'in a year or two'.

The naivety began to shatter as I tried to shift certain unnatural habits in a student's body or breath. A seemingly simple shift took such a concentrated and determined effort. I began to realize profound shifts are hard.

It dawned on me: if you had a habit of power for thousands of years it would be a world war of a struggle for men to let go without a fight.

It was in the late 1980s when a more sinister movement rolled into action.

The media took the idea of women's power and threw out images and ideas that encouraged the world to think that female strength was cosmetic. That the outside of a woman was more important than the inside.

Image was physically weakening women. You *power dressed* for power. You *sexualized* yourself for power.

Clothes, behaviour, pornography and weight loss was again trapping and locking our voices and bodies, and therefore our ability to sound and look powerful was scuppered. The relentless age of perfection and narcissism dawned in the 1990s, encasing women and some men.

Our looks more important than our content, stupidity sexier than intelligence, meanness more effective than knowledge and dignity.

I saw the relentless age of perfection encasing us from the outside.

Some women have walked a higher road with a deeper understanding, and have moved into leading positions with dignity, not duped by this trap. Some have balanced their image with their true presence, power and voice.

These women do not expect sympathetic listeners. They know that they have to communicate well and fully. They know that if they choose to use a mask it could end badly. They know that good leadership is a rare skill and requires extraordinary dedication and work.

True leaders, both women and men, seeking fairness and balance in their power, have found their place on the fulcrum of the see-saw. A balancing act that is constant and has to include juggling with their male and female energies. Not being afraid of a place that is not entirely one thing or another, a place I think of as an otherness.

The painful result of being in the middle is that you can be attacked from both sides. There is no winning this one except by being true to your fairness and decency.

In the last forty years most women have become more tenacious, more angry, more confident, but less able to communicate. As their bodies have been cosmetically encased, their voices have anatomically responded by getting tight, harsh, gasped, high and rushed.

Imitating the worst of male habits, some have become more aggressive, they are frightened of listening, so interrupt, and have replaced clear and concise debate for put-downs and insults. They resort to cynicism instead of generosity.

I have done these things and even as I did them, I knew deep down they didn't work or help me communicate constructively.

Equal exchanges require fully present listening from both parties and constitute mature exchange. When we enter a debate with anyone we have to be open to changing our mind and admitting we might be wrong, even by a degree. If not, there is no chance for change.

This is a critical time in leadership and the health of the planet.

The female spirit has been strong and resilient and has survived thousands of years of sustained attack on women's bodies, voices and stories.

It is a miracle we have survived.

It has taken its toll through millennia: the blockages in our bodies and breath so known that we feel we are vocally disempowered. Our stories bound so tightly for so long that they feel irrelevant.

But there is something we can do. We can, with hard work, change our voice. We can stay present even when we want to hide. We can lead, heal and be healed: change the course of the planet.

3
BRILLIANT WOMEN

It is requir'd you do awake your faith.

Paulina: *A Winter's Tale*

Brilliant, powerful women walk into my studio to work on their voices. Women who want recognized equality to lead. Women who have important ideas, deep wisdom and knowledge. Women with imagination and empathy who only want to be taken seriously and be heard.

They come because their voices are not serving them, they go shrill, they're not audible, their mouths struggling to make a point or the words tumbling out in a surge of incomprehensibility. They come in, and along the way, they admit or say: 'I am much more interesting than I sound.'

What does that mean? To feel that you are more interesting than you sound?

At first you feel that your insights, knowledge, experience and stories are important, but they are not appreciated or are even ignored. This is an aggressive act on the part of the listener to deny you. Whatever you do will fall on deaf ears. These non-listeners do not feel you are worth listening to.

But even if you have an attentive and sympathetic audience, so often your fear, and your unused and habitually rusty voice, cannot physically move to fully express what you want to say.

The human voice is a complex physical and muscular activity that needs constant work and care to perform well, especially when you are speaking important ideas and words.

These important ideas require a sense of authority and formality that require the speaker to be present, breathe fully and release the voice fully.

Historically, women have been viewed as speakers of non-important issues. They can be allowed to speak to encourage the ideas of men, to enjoy gossip and chit-chat, but not speak about matters of state, of crisis and of reason with gravitas.

It cannot be underestimated how these old ghosts still haunt women and impair their confidence when they stand in the spotlight.

My work begins in the realm of embodiment. For the voice to work expressively, it has to be used every day. It is that simple.

It is no accident that the privileged still have an education that teaches them how to use their voice fully in classes on a daily basis. Every child should be encouraged to do this to keep their natural voice alive.

I cannot see that social mobility is possible without every child re-engaging with their voice. It is no accident that the privileged leaders speak well but often have no content. The direct opposite to the women who walk into a room knowing that they are more interesting than they sound.

There are degrees of being interesting. You can't be interesting if you are not heard, or even if you are heard but the quality of your voice distresses the listener. This is not about accent, which is an elitist judgement, but about tone, pace and rhythm.

Tone is the quality of your voice, which is affected if it is pushed or moves up into a high note and gets stuck up there. The tone of your voice should match the content, which it can't do if the voice is tight. A weak voice has no breath. A monotonous voice has a falling rhythm. It's impossible to focus on a voice that is rushed or mumbled.

These common vocal habits appear more vividly when women are presenting or speaking formally.

All these habits start in the body, move into the breath, and into the voice and speech.

The content trapped in the speaker, or too forcefully pushed out, and the resulting effortful tone not matching your intent.

If you push, you sound aggressive even if you are feeling tender. If you rush, you sound scared or lacking in authority. If you are on half voice, a near whisper, you sound kind but a pushover. If the line falls away you sound pessimistic or bored.

If you are not present and don't make contact with the audience, then the listeners cannot be present.

You will only sound as interesting as you are when your voice sounds appropriate to what you are thinking and feeling. A balance that every professional speaker seeks.

As I've said, the vast majority of humans are born present, and with strong, flexible and free bodies and voices.

The forces of lifestyle, diet, technology, urbanization, destruction of communities, fashion and a paucity of speaking time in families, along with no spoken learning in schools, means that many human voices have suffered in the past forty years. But the voices of women have suffered most. We have the long shadow of history over us. Teaching a woman to free their voice and refind their full power takes more effort, time, work and grief than the majority of men I teach experience.

I never openly comment on this, but I work patiently to get every student and client to a place of growth, and yet groups notice, sometimes, that I am working longer with the women.

The work takes longer to consolidate because the damage is deeper in women and it starts earlier.

I have recently started to ask students to look at photos of themselves as children to see if they can spot in their photos when their inhibiting, physical habits started.

Female students see this as early as five.

Men often can't find a moment when they are not fully centred, but if they do, it's later, around the age of thirteen.

There are natural differences between the male and female voice but not enough to scupper a female speaker.

Size is the issue here! As we reach adulthood, the male larynx is larger and the vocal folds longer and thicker, between 1.75 centimetres and 2.5 centimetres in length, compared to female folds, which are 1.25 centimetres and 1.75 centimetres in length. The larger folds mean a lower pitch, but there are crossovers: a contralto female voice overlaps with a male tenor.

Generally, men have larger ribcages, so there is potential for a more powerful breath support system and consequently a louder voice. However, women have very strong lower abdominal muscles. Their hips are wider and therefore a lower breath is possible, which gives the female voice the potential for enormous power and vocal richness. The word *woman* comes from *womb* and the woman-sound is from there, as opposed to a girl's voice, which lacks that womb-richness and comes from a higher placed breath.

The bigger resonating cavities in a man's body – chest, neck, face, nose and head – amplify the male voice more. But not all men are built like this and many women are.

These size issues have an impact for heightened vocal use – for example singing opera – but for most women the natural differences are not extreme.

There is no significant difference in our voices to prevent us speaking sacred texts or great poetry.

There is no reason for a woman's natural, free voice not to be heard: for her to be shrill, shriek, to have a voice go up and not come down, to rush, to not have richness and resonance. No reason to not have a voice that can delight the listener.

The only reasons are the unnatural tensions thrown onto our bodies, into our breath systems and voice. The tensions from the outside. The mocking, the scorn, the pacifying, the oppression, the taming of our power. And the other enemy, the self-doubts and grief that the outside tensions breed in us.

We are attacked from the outside and then attack ourselves from the inside.

However distorted or held our voices, we all have moments when we feel and hear our natural voice. A full laugh until the rusty ribs begin to move again, laughing until they ache with work.

A full weep does the same thing, making our bodies aware that we have a fully active breath system.

Then there are the moments when we voice or speak out under duress. We feel so much that we refind our voice and innate articulacy.

The moments that male tyrants, bullies and predators dread are the moments when a woman's outrage is so huge that any vocal reduction drops away from her and her full vocal power is revealed.

It is worth noting that if women are corseted – and this could also be very tight clothing – in these moments preventing the ribs to fully engage and take in breath, they will faint, pass out with the trapped emotion.

This is the point when male tyrants, if they don't have the power to kill the woman, will call her mad or hysterical, show their disgust at her ugliness and call her rage 'nasty'.

A story from one of my trained teachers. A petite woman but someone with such a work ethic that she sounds, if you didn't see her, enormous. She has ambitiously tapped into her full vocal potential and worked to sustain it.

This event happened before we met and probably gave her insight into her full power.

Lacey had no substantial voice work before this story happened.

She was nineteen. A small, Hawaiian woman, walking in early evening to visit a friend. She got lost and gradually realized that she was being followed by a large man. She became very present and tried to strategically lose him or find someone in the street to help.

His stalking of her continued for some time. No one to help her. He was getting closer.

As he became very close she turned and faced him. He smirked and said, 'Bitch.' At that moment she took the deepest breath she had ever consciously taken and let out a sound so huge and free that she didn't feel it in her throat. The force of the sound threw him back and knocked him to the ground. He got up and ran away, terrified. How did she do this? How was he knocked over? The physical energy of her voice winded him, or the shock of such a sound coming from such a petite girl derailed him – or both.

This story is not uncommon.

4
WHOLE PRESENCE, WHOLE VOICE

Nothing will come of nothing.

King Lear

The whole presence

Oppressors do not want whole presence from anyone not considered their equal.

For women this is complex. Punished for full presence when it shows their intelligence, but rewarded when their presence is to please, engage in sexual flirting and often when being silly.

Whole presence is vividly seen through the eyes looking out at the world and many women are frightened of looking out and being seen.

This loss of presence has to be refound.

Presence is the energy that is the life force in us all. We cannot survive without presence; even when we have drenched it out with alcohol or drugs, we can feel our focus awaken through our dimmed selves when threatened.

Presence is meshed into our bodies, breath and voice. Presence ignites our hearts, our minds, our curiosity and our interest in the world around us. It is the source of an individual's inside world reaching out and connecting with all around them.

It is a circle of energy that fully surrounds us, and although we see it in each other's eyes, it flows out of every part of us.

When your presence meets another human's you are connected and have a chance to understand each other. And when this exchange happens, two doors are opened. There is a two-way passage of energy between you: give and take. There is balance, and within that exchange there is equality. Even if one person has more power, there is acknowledgement of a shared meeting and humanity. Even a leader meeting and sharing presence with you for a few seconds: you feel you are known and seen and equal.

When we are fully present we have two simultaneous connections with the world. One connection is with the whole group or space around you, and the other connection is with one person in the group or a point in the space – both of these connections might be only fleeting.

For example, a baby is looking into the eyes of its parent but is also aware of a cat arriving in the room.

An actor speaking to another actor on stage should be present to the actor and to the audience, even if they are not looking at them. The actor listening should also give their full presence to the speaking actor and the audience.

The presence, to a single point, is used when we attend to a task, but we should be aware that there might be danger around us. If the task is performed and the rest of the world is not in our 360 degree presence, we get lost in our actions, and therefore have to return to the world around us after finishing it. These all-absorbing and blinkered activities are only safely carried out when you are in a secure place. This is our double, natural, energetic capability and in some societies I have worked with, it is still thriving.

Urbanization and technology in Western civilization have threatened to wipe out our presence to each other and the group.

The Zulus know how to stay present as they cross a dangerous landscape but also meet each other with the greeting 'See me?' asked of a stranger.

'I see you,' as the stranger becomes present to them.

The extinction of communities, families and the profound loneliness many feel is the result of the loss of our 360 degree presence.

In the late 1970s, I started to develop what I now term the 'Three Circles of Energy', as I had noticed that students were not as present as they should be and couldn't form a group or harness their full attention and power.

I began to understand that not being present impacted the body, breath and voice, and more profoundly our sensitivity, curiosity and awareness of the world.

When a student was fully present, the body had a chance to naturally align, and the voice be free and released. I began to call this position *A State of Readiness*, and it's what I now term Second Circle. In this state you are in the moment. In the now.

Students who were slumped, looking down, walking without purpose, with shallow breathing, voice falling back into themselves, muttered, de-energized, eyes disengaged – a state I had previously termed *Denial* – is now what I call First Circle. I noticed that this habit of withdrawal, which results in a lack of presence, was mostly a female position. In this state you are falling back into the past.

Other students – then mostly male – adopted a position I'd thought of as *Bluff*: now Third Circle. A forced, pushed-out position – chest up, chin up, legs locked, breath over-controlled, voice too loud. In this state you are pushing yourself into the future. A pretence of power, but in some ways as weak as First Circle because both inhibit the natural breath, and put you in danger. Both *Denial* and *Bluff* cut off your sensitivity to the world around you. You are not conscious of yourself or your surroundings. In the 1980s, women began to adopt *Bluff* – Third Circle – as they mimicked the male's bad habits of force and pretence.

As you enter a room, long before you speak, the way you look and breathe alerts the animal in all of us, and we know whether you have authority and are due respect.

We know whether you are authentically powerful if the body and walk is centred, the eyes looking with presence and curiosity, and the breath is fully connected to the lower abdominal muscles and is not rushed or gasped. The jaw is not clenched. Energy is leaving you and our energy enters. You give out energy and receive it with your full presence.

Most are born within their full presence and within that energy a full potential to be alive, curious and great. Those that have maintained it walk into the world without the clutter of fear but with the freedom bestowed on them by loving guardians.

In this way, for millennia, a privileged boy who has been consistently fully acknowledged (in other words, unconditionally loved) appears to be, and often is, unstoppable.

A privileged boy who has not has the acceptance of unconditional love, appears to be confident but is often a dangerous energy to himself and those around him. He's not fully present: he's pretending to be.

On the other hand, an unprivileged boy filled with unconditional love can break through the barriers of his beginnings and surface into power.

These boys walk out into the world with presence, and will be respected. However, girls mostly meet the opposite reaction to their full power: it is not respected, but attacked. Women are punished for being too present. Punished for not being present enough. Mocked when their presence has gravitas.

In many rooms it is easier for a girl not to be present, but to close down to stop these attacks or unwanted sexual attention.

A girl's full presence is still dangerous to many. Some men (and women) still encourage girls to withdraw, to not show the world their presence – this can be a strategy for survival and is intended to lovingly protect the girl child. This protection is a good thing if it doesn't erode their ability to return to their natural presence.

This book explores how women can return to their whole presence and power.

The whole voice

Our natural presence and voice are linked. They're each reliant on the other. Any blockage in presence affects our voice and any blockage in our voice affects our presence.

The marriage of presence and voice is housed in, and is reliant upon, a centred and aligned body. An efficient body that doesn't carry useless tensions in the feet, through the legs, pelvic area, stomach, spine, upper chest and shoulders, neck and jaw.

A stance, walk and run of complete effortless energy throughout the body, with that energy, and appropriate tensions, constantly changing to fulfil particular physical actions.

Our natural state doesn't waste energy. The energy should be appropriate to the task being performed; the lifting of a heavy case, or of a feather.

The state of our body affects the breath. The breath powers everything in us, including the voice.

The natural breath should have no tension or lift of the shoulders, upper chest or jaw. As we breathe in, the ribs should open at the sides and back of the ribcage, and then there should be a release of muscles down to the groin.

As we breathe out, the muscles that control our breath from the deepest place in our bodies and around the ribcage should move in to create a column of air that supports or powers the body, voice, brain and heart. If we cannot breathe fully we cannot be wholly present. We cannot think, feel or be fully heard and taken seriously.

The flow and strength of the breath changes with whatever task needs to be performed. The bigger the rock that needs moving, the bigger the breath. The bigger the space we're speaking in, the bigger the breath.

The louder the sound, the bigger the breath used to power the voice. And breath should be under every sound we make.

The breath should support a free voice that releases without blockage from our mouth. The breath and free voice will change note and range to express our thoughts and feelings.

Sound and tone should express what is being said.

Blockages in the voice warp the exact meaning of what we are attempting to say, because the quality of the voice does not match the words.

As the voice moves out into the world, the speech muscles should effortlessly mould the voice into words.

A natural presence and voice is what we associate with authentic authority and power. The Alpha leader is *in* and *with* their presence, body and voice, and their power is effortless and appropriate to whatever they are doing or communicating.

I have met many Alpha men who have never had to work on themselves. I have met Alpha women, but they have all had to reconnect through hard effort to their natural power and leadership rights. Women still find this in flashes, but the ones I have met have not been able to do this in a sustained way that can find consistency in a leadership role without work.

In prehistory these women ruled as equals, as they still do in many indigenous communities. But these were the women early civilizations hunted down, tamed or stoned to death.

I have spent considerable time in my career studying apes. In order to help actors become chimpanzees, gorillas and bonobos, I have watched and discussed their behaviour with experts, noticed their physicality and their voices, and generally observed how power works in their energy and the community's energy.

The remarkable Ailsa Berk in the film, *Greystroke* (1983), had to go through this transformation. She was playing Tarzan's adopted mother – an ape – and we developed a working dialogue as to how, under her quarter-of-a-million-dollar ape costume, she could fully fill, authentically, the being underneath the cosmetic mask. With Ailsa I worked to help her animate from within and bring life to her costume.

This involved much research and visits to communities of apes.

Other ape films came along, and my study was highly enhanced with the work I did on *Walking with Cavemen* (BBC/the Discovery Channel) in 2002.

I was continually chipping away at the Circles and in observation of gorillas and chimps I made joyous discoveries.

Alpha males and females sit centred and keenly observant of their community, attentive and quick to intervene with appropriate power in any disturbance. They keep the peace. They move efficiently and economically across the space, and give exactly the right physical punishment to any wrongdoing, not too hard and not too soft. Alongside their actions there is always a stillness and a fairness. They vocalize when needed and always appropriately. Their centred efficiency and vocal economy is the hub of the group.

My real delight was the observations I made around those wanting power and those not wanting power.

The young males – not yet Alphas but trying to be – are puffed up, bouncing around, making a lot of noise, mess, throwing things, and braying and hooting.

A full caricature of Third Circle Bluff.

All were seeking power but were not the Alpha. The Alpha could and did give a well-timed whack and the challenge disappeared. One would eventually unseat the Alpha and would then adopt the still, balanced and efficient use of power that made the whole group safe.

The loud chaotic, bluffing young ape is not a safe or creative leader who has the group's survival and well-being in mind. The group needs that young, aggressive and unstrategic energy to be utilized to protect the group, not lead it.

There are males in the group who do not want leadership. They are happy to be part of the group and will display First Circle withdrawal when challenged or noticed. They know their comfort zone and do not move outside it. They might be males who have challenged and failed, or those who never wanted leadership. The group will tolerate them as long as they stay in a conciliatory low-key presence.

The female Alpha performs a similar role, checking any female troublemakers. The same centred power, the same appropriate energy for any group misdemeanour.

The female Alpha is not loyal or sentimental when there is a change of power. For the safety of her offspring and perhaps the well-being of the community, she will change allegiances when the male Alpha falls, and when her breeding years are over she can still hold court and have respect in the group.

I viewed this behaviour as an amateur with a purpose. I'm not a scientist, and my views were subjective, but these encounters with apes in these protected communities gave me important insights into behaviour, and the creative and healthy leadership of a group.

While rehearsing with Ailsa, I had noticed many human behaviours that were everyday but now had powerful implications on my work.

In a restaurant I watched with amusement as the Third Circle man tried desperately to call the waiter. Clicking fingers, waving an arm. This might have worked with a less mature and experienced waiter, but this one had found his own Second Circle-centred power, and although not a wealthy man, wasn't going to be clicked at by a bluffing male customer.

However, this waiter responded immediately to the really powerful man in the restaurant. He only had to lift his head up and glance towards the waiter to get his fast attention. This was the real Alpha even though he was less expensively dressed than the young bluffer.

The pattern continued with the women. One could get the attention in the same underplayed and centred way. Another waving woman was similarly ignored for a time.

These observations stimulated my imagination around the work. The group all know what real power is by the way we use energy in body and voice.

I watched and experimented.

The crush at the bar to buy a drink.

The men waving their tenners and raising their voices got service before me, but after the quiet, still, centred men – that economic 'don't mess with me' energy.

Like many women, I was angry at not being served, and often found myself getting vocally aggressive, which also didn't work. So I changed tactics. I had the tenner in my hand. Didn't wave it, stayed very present and focused on the bartender.

I started to get served before the Third Circle men but not before the Second Circle-centred men. This applied with male and female bartenders. Interesting.

My success was so apparent to the Third Circle men waving their money that I started to get verbally abused, and although I didn't push in, I was often accused of doing so. They did not challenge the Second Circle men served before them in the same way.

This was a powerful experiment for me, but I still often felt shame, humiliation and sadness for being at the bar, playing their games, but ultimately illustrating to myself my own 'inequality'.

What would it be like to inhabit a body and voice that had been unquestionably deemed equal?

5
THE UNQUESTIONABLY EQUAL WOMAN

No coward soul is mine,
No trembler in the world's storm-troubled sphere:
I see Heaven's glories shine,
And faith shines equal, arming me from Fear.

Emily Brontë

A woman fully present and not frightened of looking without hesitation or being seen without shame.

A woman in any time or any environment.

She would know that she was not safe in a wilderness or in a Wall Street bank. Her eyes would really look around her and ears really hear. She would not expect protection if alone. Eyes not cast down at the path unless she sensed a snake, but she would still be centred in that 360 degree awareness.

She would move forward if she needed to without hesitation or apology. Her instincts would allow her to do what she needed to do, not to comply with how she had been told to behave.

She would yield backwards if she felt she was in danger from a predator. She would not flatter by allowing a predator too close or laugh at an unfunny joke. She would instinctively know the right spatial distance required. She would not stay in a place that made her feel uncomfortable. If someone was too close or moving in on her, she would move away. She wouldn't stay close to someone who could do her harm.

If need be she could run fully, with economy and efficiency making her fast. She could climb or hurl a rock with strength and accuracy.

She hasn't listened to anyone who has told her that these activities are unladylike.

She has full balance.

This means she allows her body its natural design. The natural placement has not been distorted by habits that take away her power. She stands with her feet on the floor, the weight slightly on the balls of her feet. Ankles free, knees unlocked, pelvis on top of the legs, not pushed forward or pulled back.

She knows without thinking that her breath has to go low into her body to engage her full physical and vocal power.

Her spine is up. Not slumped or too rigid. It is the centre of her physical structure and needs to be placed properly, so it doesn't stop her breath or signal to the world that she is weak.

Her shoulders and upper chest are released. Not lifted or rounded – that would stop the breath and power, and interfere with how she deals with fear. The upper chest tensions move fear into panic.

Her head is at the top of her spine, not tucked in or pushed forward, so she can see the world well, look around, not only down, when necessary.

Her jaw is not clenched except when – for a fraction of a second – she needs *flight or fight*. The teeth clench for a moment, to gather the breath enough to run or hit, but this is inefficient for long stretches of time. Even that clenching is a waste of energy; and power does not waste energy. Not only does inefficient tension deplete us, but it desensitizes us to the world around us and inside us.

She knows that the two major power points in the body are the balls of the feet connected to the earth, and the lower abdominal muscles that can activate the power of her body, breath and voice.

She will not tolerate any tension that distorts her power, which is the channel of energy from her feet, located in the lower breath and expelled through her open mouth – with or without sound. She has re-remembered this by pushing a rock against a wall. It can't be done efficiently without the feet and the lower breath being fully engaged. Shoulder tensions, like those in the jaw, weaken her.

She also needs to be able to turn and move quickly through her feet, and any useless ankle, knee or pelvic tension slows her down.

Of course she can employ choice around her power. She can lessen her physical power so that she doesn't frighten anyone. She can even do it to attract someone. But it's a choice.

She knows that if she wears her favourite high-heeled shoes or tight-fitting bodice, she is putting her power at risk and is ready to kick off those shoes and rip her bodice if she needs to run or fight.

I believe most women have felt this physical freedom. A clear need to survive can unbind our habits rapidly. This could be by an aggressive attack, or one of those silly dances we do down the street when we trip over. In the attempt to not fall, in those few embarrassing seconds through the dance, the body has discarded our physical distortions; and when we come to rest we suddenly feel physically more centred and connected.

Breath and voice

Our present woman's breath connects to her body.

Her voice is free and leaves her.

She takes breaths fully and silently. She doesn't gasp, as that will give the predator an advantage. Not only can her presence be heard, but the predator knows that a gasp is a small, high-chested breath that displays weakness.

She knows men interrupt when women gasp.

She knows without thought that her power is dependent on her opening her ribs and allowing her abdominal muscles to release down into the groin.

Her stomach will move out, not flop out, but be noticed as the breath moves it.

If she wants to hold her stomach in she knows the risks. It will weaken her. It will stop her voice being rich and powerful.

The holding in of the stomach not only restricts the breath power, but is connected to the throat and closes it, so the voice moves up in pitch. She wants and needs her power, so she won't exercise the stomach muscles so that they become so tight that her power is lost.

She knows that her authority – taking the power she needs, through breath – is reliant on her acting or speaking when she is ready. Not speaking before the breath is there. Or after.

She will move and vocalize in the moment.

She takes what she needs in breath. The action required is linked to the amount of breath she needs to take. The larger the space she is speaking in, the more passion of thought or feeling, the more breath.

She never stints herself or, more importantly, allows men to suffocate her with their presence.

Her voice is free and placed out of her. It carries itself on the breath and has free passage. No locks in the throat or mouth. An arc of sound unashamedly travelling through space. She doesn't pull back, swallow or bluff her voice into the pretend power of push, or false deepening of her pitch. She doesn't need to rush. She doesn't laugh at herself.

Her facial muscles are not held or the jaw locked into a frown or smile. She owns her face, and after any expression her face returns to neutral.

She is free and unfettered.

In prehistory she would have been honoured as an Alpha woman.

We have not named her here, because these women are never named. Think of the witches in Macbeth.

Boy/men

A Second Circle Alpha man uses his strength to protect those in his care, not attack them. Comfortable in his position, he enjoys the company of powerful people, which includes powerful women, as equals.

But there are men who have a fear around their masculinity that makes it impossible for them to accept the equality of the women around them.

The first time I heard the term 'boy/man' was from a SAS leader I was coaching in the 1980s. I have always enjoyed teaching powerful men. There is no turmoil for a woman when she's with a man who accepts her equality. That doesn't mean we don't debate and disagree; but we avoid diminishing the power or authenticity in each other. The women's equality is not questioned, flattered or demeaned, and the woman is not frightened of the man's power.

This conversation with the SAS leader led to him saying, ' . . . Well, that's because we're not *boys/men*.' I immediately understood the men he was describing.

The ape observations were also relevant at this moment: young apes bouncing about in Third Circle bluff, challenging the really powerful, balanced Alpha. Using force and bullying to crash around the compound, destroying the space and trying to destroy the group.

There have always been *boys/men*, but in the 1980s it became fashionable to promote them, and eventually to allow them to lead. Suddenly, these leaders were not grown up and were not being responsible, and this went hand in hand with greed and narcissism.

Some women imitated Third Circle, and also pushed for power, hung out with the lads, drank with them, slept with them, bullied with them and destroyed groups with them.

Other women moving into power chose the opposite route: they withdrew into First Circle, only noticed when they were needed. These women gathered information, data, networks and strategies. No one can feel safe around a Third Circle leader. When you are being led by a *boy/man*, a woman's Second Circle presence has to be hidden. They have to disguise their power, intelligence and talent.

Women have learnt to perform for men who have power over them, which is exhausting, demeaning and humiliating. They please men with a 'girl's' voice, smiling, laughing at their jokes, not pushing the hand off their thigh and not backing away when they can't bear the bad breath.

These habits are ones adopted for survival.

When the *boy/man* discovers this simple technique, they feel they have been duped, and punish us for it.

Shakespeare not only gives his women words and ideas that prove them equal, but he shows how immature male power destroys all. That misuse of power often starts with the destruction of a woman who speaks the truth.

In *King Lear*, Lear exiles his favourite daughter, Cordelia, for telling the truth. He is a *boy/man* at the age of eighty. He wants to be liked, plays games, and although he has some fine leadership qualities, he wants it all. An army without responsibility, and to break the laws of inheritance to suit his comfortable place in the world.

He has a terrible journey to learn the lessons of humility and fairness. He has to realize that his actions against his daughters were wrong, and the last utterances that he makes are to say *please* and *thank you*.

Women in positions of power must not be tempted to imitate the behaviour of *boys/men*.

Although they are mocked by these men for being serious, thorough, authentic and dedicated, they must resist being 'one of the lads' who hasn't grown up, and one of the hardened lads who cannot be vulnerable enough to say, 'Sorry, I was wrong.'

Taming

We know that there was an ancient time when women were equal to men. Women shared equal power in leadership and both had political and spiritual power.

The beginning of urbanization, paving over nature, building walls, building roads, building mighty armies to conquer, was almost certainly the beginning of the end of women's equality. Women who continued to exercise power were hunted down, burnt and stoned. Beautiful and precious women were pampered and stroked into submission, tended with so much care and conditional love that some were made decadent and unable to look after themselves.

These women believe they are safe when they are not. They are often rewarded for being needy. Women guarded by men joined men in the hatred of strong women.

It still benefits some women to be tamed. Particularly if they are tamed by a wealthy man.

I think about those beautiful, fluffy cats you find in warm, cosy houses. Rarely leaving the house, maybe a waddle around the garden, with no chance of ever catching a bird.

I first saw one of these cats when I was six, in a house in Primrose Hill that was owned by a colleague of my father's. I was fascinated with how safe it must have felt with no memory of a threat. But it was more intriguing. It's cosy, threatless life had dampened its natural survival instincts.

The cat entranced me as it slept with its paws tucked under its chin. It was not a scared or alert creature. No need for a quick dart of a claw. Observing and knowing all about the house, the comings and goings, without fear and without a need to ever attack. To me, a boring cat. No fire, but complacent and presumably content. Tamed into meekness.

Very unlike the wild cat my brother brought home from school as a kitten. The claw always a possibility, as was the aerial attack you could suffer as you went up the staircase. Definitely never tamed, which is why he was called Oscar. Oscar Wilde. But my mother, who loved that cat, was never clawed. I think my mother felt tamed, and should have been allowed her claws in the world.

For some women there isn't the privilege of the adoration of a man or his wealth to tolerate tameness. They have to face the hatred of men for their wildness, or hide and mask their power with strategies that can include forms of deception.

All this exhausting effort has to be performed when we are not thought of as equal.

6
EQUAL?

I think I was six when my child's mind first asked this question – *Are girls equal?* – again and again. I asked teachers, my mother and friends. It wasn't a debate anyone in my circle seemed to want before the mid-seventies, but I was plagued by it.

When I was eight, at my mixed school I liked playing with the boys. The games were better. The boys treated me with muted interest, but I was pushed out of some conversations and activities.

I gave my usual cry of 'It's not fair!' when I wasn't allowed to ride one boy's scooter. That call engaged the four boys who had been allowed to ride it. They shared that particular male smirk all women have seen, and then they turned on me.

'It's fair because boys are better than girls.'

'Why?'

Laughter. 'You're a *girl*.'

'But I beat you at rounders! I get better marks than you.'

The laughter increased.

'If boys want to kill you they can.' This was Charles, the leader of the boys. 'Boys are better because we are stronger.'

This, then, was an important clue to the equality question. It was a piece of the fairness jigsaw that enlightened and worried me.

This was worth spending thinking time on. And the first thing that came to me was: *But some boys, some men are not physically strong.* I had wrestled a boy neighbour to the ground only a few weeks ago.

Some of my father's important friends were very weak looking. One shook hands with a wet grip, one couldn't swim when he visited us on holiday and screamed when a wave knocked him off his feet in the shallows.

Could it be possible that this idea of physical prowess had given men the idea they were better than us?

I picked and then dug at this problem. Not *all* men were physically strong. The idea was not consistent.

Then, a visit to London Zoo.

There was a gorilla named Guy, a famous inmate of Regents Park Zoo. I stood transfixed by this wondrous animal. His power, his physical ease and his fearless gaze moved my heart.

I had the answer for Charles.

As soon as was possible I confronted him.

'Charles, do you think that because you're strong, you're better than girls?'

'Yes!' Big grin.

'Then it means that Guy the Gorilla is more important than any man. Guy could beat any man with one push. Pull *your* arm out with a tug.'

Charles faltered. I knew I had won. He was unsure and agitated, his mind working hard.

'No he wouldn't. I'd shoot him. Men invented guns.'

'That's not you being stronger. It's a gun and women can shoot too. Women can hold a gun.'

I was triumphant and walked away.

Before I knew what was happening, I was pushed over from behind onto my stomach, my dress pulled up and my pants pulled down exposing my bottom.

'I hope the whole world can see your stupid bottom!'

Charles's coda to our argument. He stomped off, not fully triumphant. He was right that as he pushed me down and pulled my skirt up and my pants down I could not resist. But I knew I was right and something was understood.

This episode with Charles was not a bad, scarring experience, but all women have had an encounter with a Charles.

Some women endure life-threatening and disgusting encounters with men on a daily basis. Many are raped and killed.

It was an event years ago that made me realize that so many privileged men rarely, if ever, experience humiliating acts or words to their face. They are not harmed in a way that threatens them. They might have spats over supper, but they walk away with these remarks splashing off them like water off a duck's back. These spats may hurt, but they don't threaten physical destruction.

Years ago I was working at the Royal National Theatre (RNT), sitting with three directors, one a man. He had arrived late and was visibly shaken. After a while he told us that he had been verbally attacked on his way to the theatre. He had bumped into a large man who had taken against him as 'an upper-class shit'.

We gave him comfort, but later, after the two other women had left, he complained to me that we hadn't displayed sufficient shock or sympathy.

'Is this the first time these types of comments have been made to you?' I asked.

'Yes!'

I explained that for most women, his experience was a regular one. He was in his forties, white, upper class and very privileged, and had never had threatening words spoken to him. He was brilliant, but not physically large or strong, and yet had managed to live until then without a stranger humiliating, threatening or even patronizing him.

Men have convinced women and themselves that it is their physical strength over us – even the women that could floor them – that gives them superiority. Even the physically weak men believe this or feel so sure of themselves that they know we cannot act against them.

I can still see the battle in some young men who are troubled by being taught by a woman who has authority over them.

As I grow older, the challenges becomes more subtle, but the threat of the possibility of violence still continues.

Physical strength did not give human beings the ability to conquer the planet. This is what did:

The human mind – intelligence, strategy, the ability to build tools.

The human heart – emotional intelligence that can build families and communities.

The capacity to work together as a team.

And the language that could express and understand the past, the present and the future, and tell stories to remember knowledge, educate and structure human morality.

These are the skills that gave humans the earth. Not physical muscle.

Women are equal to men in all the skills that give us dominance over nature. In many areas they are often better! As a generalization, we can build communities and teams better than most men. We collaborate more readily.

If we were reliant on male, physical prowess to rule the planet, then prides of lions, encounters with gorillas and packs of wild dogs would have wiped us out long before that sense of superiority firstly squashed women and then challenged the power of nature.

A bushman who guided me when I was working on a film in the Kalahari told me that a group of four 12-year-olds can deal with a lion, using their strategic thinking and team work. An individual, however strong, would be slaughtered.

He also told me that if a rhino charged at us, to run in a zig-zag, as their eyes are set in a way that can only follow a straight line and turning quickly is not in the structure of their body.

'How did you find that out?' I asked.

His reply: 'It's all in the stories about rhinos.'

'Who tells these stories?'

'The women. The women notice these things and tell us.'

Physical power doesn't build communities and societies that are inclusive. As this power was misused, it not only brutalized women, but was used to destroy civilizations more in tune with nature and the inclusivity of women. Western civilization is based on one of the most violent and savage empires, the Roman Empire, which took the worshipping of physical force to a new level, crushing the more sensitive and balanced communities around them.

As men misused their physical force over women and children, they came to assume that they had intellectual and spiritual superiority. This strategy only worked if women were denied knowledge and roles in the sacred rituals.

It is always wonderfully sad but funny to see a small, physically weak man believing that he can hold court over a group of brilliant women; and protected by the law, he could. An old, weak man could, and sometimes still can order the stoning of a young, vibrant girl to death. But it hasn't and won't work. It hasn't stopped women from surfacing. Using their bodies, minds and spirits to survive this male force and to learn defence strategies to survive; and then frequently surpassing men in their knowledge and artistry, even when they knew they would be punished.

And if these brilliant women survived punishment, their works were forgotten when they died or were stolen from them and plagiarized by men.

Which brings me onto the two brilliant women who brought me up.

7
MOTHER MARGARET AND NANNA WINIFRED

Margaret

When I hear friends describe their mothers I understand how overwhelmingly blessed I have been.

Margaret was a sweet, kind, attentive and profoundly decent woman and mother. She was there in the morning, and there to welcome us whenever we returned home. Even awake, watching from a window, when I left an abusive relationship and phoned to tell her. There she was at 3.00 am waiting and she was quick to make a cup of tea.

Not a physically demonstrative mother but a fully present one.

I taught her to hug when I was eighteen. And after the first few – accompanied by her laughter – she was so happy to receive and return the embraace.

Margaret didn't have a public voice: she had a private one. She was a listener, but when offered the space to express herself, could find words, ideas and clarity in what she thought and felt. But it had to be a safe place. I never heard her raise her voice, shout or swear. She would laugh until the tears rolled down her face, but without much sound. I only heard her full vocal potential two days before she died.

She was never offered a place to express important decisions or choices in her married life. I don't believe my father thought this was cruel – it was – but it never occurred to him or his friends that she might have a powerful opinion. She was a woman and working class, not well educated, and presumably she would be grateful for his mounting wealth, the expensive holidays and acquisitions.

Margaret never spent money on herself or asked for gifts, and therefore rarely got them. She did a fine job without complaining, hiding disappointment and slowly drowning in depression caused by her husband's neglect.

He could never understand why she wasn't delighted when he announced a first-class cruise.

'You didn't ask her!' – My response to his dismay and my defence of her. 'You didn't give her a choice.' My explanation.

His eyes blank, he was unwilling to hear what he thought was an idealistic, immature attack from his own daughter.

He had performed these strategies all their married life. He arrived home to their council flat in Pimlico, announcing that he had bought a house in the suburbs, forensically removing her and her mother, my nanna, from their friends and memories to a house among the middle classes. A place alien to both of them. But *he* could drive and leave suburbia for his work and life without us, in London. Although he loved her, it was very apparent that he found her class a problem, and he never gave her status in public and never defended her when his friends ignored her. Her new, middle-class social circle quickly became aware of this.

Margaret never felt at home with the 'posh' women and our friends' mothers. She saw them very clearly and endured their pretensions, observing it all with her wry amusement. Never cruel, just a sense of the ridiculous and a kindness to let them behave in a way that comforted them. The wearing of a cocktail hat, the predecessor of the 1980s 'fascinator' – so silly on the head of a visitor drinking my mother's always perfectly made cuppa and delicately eating a slice of her Victoria sponge. So silly to watch the fluttering of feathers and imitation insects over her head, that Mother caught my eye, and the slight roll in it made me have to leave the room before I collapsed in giggles. Or not at all funny, the time I saw her patiently collect a grand friend for tea. She had learned to drive by then, so wasn't having to carry shopping for a mile. Given a car that he chose, she was a slow and safe driver, and was used by many of her posh 'friends' to ferry them to and fro.

I saw her park the car and walk around to open the door for this woman.

Later I challenged her as to why she had done that and she shrugged. 'Her husband always did that for her, it makes her feel cared for: she's a widow.'

That day I took this lady home and as we stopped outside her mansion she waited for me to do the same. 'My husband always opened the door for me.' A sweet smile, verging on a pout.

'I will open the door for you, but please don't treat my mother like a chauffeur. She is older than you and you can easily open the door.'

I never told my mother about that exchange, but it broke my heart that no-one knew her enough to give her equality. Did they tolerate her working-class roots in exchange for her kindness and generosity? They always ate well and drank good wine. My father kept a good cellar.

Nanna

My nanna, Winnie, was a harder nut to crack. Her rage was close to the surface. A tough life. She had no comfort until Margaret married and my father made money, and she became part of the family, moving in under his roof. Never directly confronting her son-in-law, but never conceding to or flattering him either. Once we moved, she lost the friends she loved in London.

She kept her secrets and her dignity. A fierce spirit who could tell a story better than most and only, in my experience, to me. She was frightening and compelling to me. I adored her, but her spirit was always dangerous.

Even in her eighties she once wrestled me to the floor, twisting my hands with hers, over the TV channel we were watching! Television was her great comfort and joy in the twentieth century. Later, shocked that I had been so easily defeated, I realized that her hands and arms had *worked* – she washed clothes for money and she proudly boasted that she was a good wringer-outer.

Her words and ideas would also wrestle me down, and she would intentionally burst my middle-class, educated pretensions. Often painful, but the impact was always creative and educational.

Once after an exchange, which she saw had hurt me, she said, 'You don't know who I am. No one here does.'

'Tell me, please.'

She outstared me. 'It's too deep and distant.' And that was the end of it.

As Bottom in *A Midsummer Night's Dream* says and knew: *Our stories have no bottom.*

Without voices and words, we cannot express ourselves to the world or to ourselves.

I think Margaret and Winnie did know themselves.

They knew their journeys and their historic limitations. They also knew the limitations set by the world of men. They understood, in their time and place, that men were unsympathetic listeners. They didn't have to listen, or care what their women thought or felt.

I have already mentioned that our house didn't have books – I never saw my father read a book, only the *Financial Times* and the magazines he published.

But there was a cupboard that I discovered with Mother's battered *The Complete Works of Shakespeare* and the *Collins Albatross Book of Verse*.

I took them to my bedroom. In fact I stole them. I hid them and read them. I was nine. I didn't want to share them, as I felt that there was guilt attached to the joy I found in reading these secret treasures. In today's terms, I was extremely uncool.

One day, my well-mannered mother knocked on my door. She never, ever walked in on any of us without a gentle tap.

I had left the poetry book out.

When she caught sight of it, I felt guilty. I knew she wouldn't punish me, but might be disappointed at my theft. I watched her eyes fill with tears as she picked it up.

She then recited from heart Leigh Hunt's '*Jenny Kiss'd Me*'.

Jenny kiss'd me when we met,
Jumping from the chair she sat in;
Time, you thief, who love to get
Sweets into your list, put that in!
Say I'm weary, say I'm sad,
Say that health and wealth have miss'd me,
Say I'm growing old, but add,
Jenny kiss'd me.

Thus began, probably, the most important bond I felt with my mother. One that no one else had. I believe I gave my mother two of the highlights of her life, when I was able to introduce her to Lady Mary Soames – the daughter of Winston Churchill, for my mother the greatest man to have lived – and Barbara Leigh Hunt: the great actor, who is a descendent of Leigh Hunt.

This secret allowed me to bring poetry books home from school and share them with her. She got it. She knew something was being filled in me by poetry. She understood something about me that no one else did, and I her. My mother loved poetry. I saw a rare thing in her when we discussed it: joy. Underneath her sweetness and kindness I had always felt a dark loneliness. It was only later I identified it as grief.

She loved laughing at silly, harmless, unhurtful things. She loved to dance, folk dances and singing robust hymns. But she found no joy in wealth or station.

She loved poems that had rhythm, and as I got older and hit that stage most thirteen-year-olds go through – the arrogance of ignorance – I thought her choice of poems simple and lacking in intellectual depth. How horrible this ignorance is, this lack of insight and sympathy.

Here is one we spoke together – Harold Monro, *Overheard on a Saltmarsh*.

'Nymph, nymph, what are your beads?'
'Green glass, goblin. Why do you stare at them?'
'Give them me.'
    'No.'
'Give them me. Give them me.'
    'No.'
'Then I will howl all night in the reeds.
Lie in the mud and howl for them.'
'Goblin, why do you love them so?'
'They are better than stars or water,
Better than voices of winds that sing,
Better than any man's fair daughter,
Your green glass beads on a silver ring.'
'Hush, I stole them out of the moon.'
'Give me your beads. I want them.'
    'No.'
'I will howl in a deep lagoon

For your green glass beads, I love them so.
Give them me. Give them.'
  'No.'

She and I thought the poem was a lovely story – as it is on the child's level – about fairies in the forest. The dark underworld was not apparent. Rather like the shock in *A Midsummer Night's Dream* when we realize how dangerous and dark Puck is. It thrilled me that the Nymph held firm. I knew her voice would be strong and clear and not reliant on his sympathy. No apology, no excuses, no compromise.

We hadn't the equality laws yet, but I knew she had an equal voice to his and had no fear of using it. The voice, I knew, came from her womb. I knew she looked at him with her full presence, no dipped head, fluttering eyes, smile or wriggling body.

Centred and focused and unafraid of repercussions.

  'No.'

Later, in 1973, when I was at the Royal Central School, I was fortunate enough to be taught by Gerard Benson – a great poet, he started *Poems on The Underground* and was a founder member of the Barrow Poets – and I heard the poem again, spoken by Gerard. I then, through the twinkle in his voice, knew that this was a complex poem about sex and consent – or lack of it.

There is no negotiation or hesitancy. It is a fearless rejection of the goblin. The Nymph is not squeaky clean! She has stolen the beads from the moon, but the poem's power lies in the sureness of what she owns and chooses not to give – beads, jewels. Women were taught, until very recently, that to give the jewel of your virginity away would ruin your life and put you at risk of never marrying at best, or a stoning at worst.

The Nymph's authoritative 'No' thrills and scares anyone who fears the potential power of the goblin. Has he more power than her? What will he do? We don't know what he does after the end of the poem, but our imaginations wander into dark places.

There are three options:

He enjoys her clarity and strength, and a powerful friendship ensues! That's the romantic hope. The path that the decent men in Shakespeare follow when challenged by an articulate woman.

Secondly, he dislikes her and will seethe, sulk and moan about her all through the salt marsh. Maybe plotting her downfall.

Or thirdly, he attacks her, takes the beads at best, or rapes her.

This last option is at the front of most woman's minds when 'No' is said to those in power. If they lose a leader's favour and protection will they consequentially be put in danger?

Women have had to learn to negotiate less clearly, to find obtuse ways of avoiding direct rejection.

For centuries men have found this strategy in women infuriating. They call it manipulative and dishonest. They have to spend hours wooing, and time flattering. They sulk and moan about how devious women are, but they are missing the point. Give us equality and rights over our own bodies and the games can stop.

Women are as direct as men and should aim to be so, but they have to feel safe and know that saying 'No' in any context will not be used against them.

But centuries of finely tuned games and habits do not disappear overnight. We will know when we are equal when directness has no retribution.

I spoke two other poems my mother loved at her funeral.

John Masefield, *Sea Fever*, and Alfred Noyes, *The Moon is Up.*

As I was reading them aloud, I realized that her favourite poems were both about escape and crossing the seas. Both about journeys away from the mediocre life that one is expected to lead.

Was she always navigating release from life or her marriage?

My mother and her mother, my nanna, from whom I felt a tough and powerful unconditional love – were the only sources from my home life from which my vocation grew, and which set me on the path that I would later pursue and dedicate my work and life to. Voice, storytelling and structured language.

After my mother's funeral, over champagne, her favourite drink, her friends gathered around me and all expressed shock that Margaret was my first connection to poetry. The Listener, in service to my father and these friends, was my inspiration. She had given me the key to the rest of my life. More sadness gathered around my heart at what they didn't know about her.

They knew Margaret as a kind, sweet, well-mannered decent woman who was supportive and who listened. But her friends had no experience of hearing her voice or her passions. They had never encountered – or as importantly – *heard* her fierce intelligence.

At the age of eleven, Margaret won a scholarship to The Grey Coat Hospital School. She once described to me how the interview went and vividly remembered the shock on the panel's faces when she answered their questions about where she lived. She told them the truth. She lived in a council room on Silver Street, off Berkeley Market. There was a curtain that divided her bed from her parents. On the lower floor, there was a block bathroom and toilet.

To their credit, they offered her a place.

She never went. Her father was frightened of the expense of the uniform, and more likely frightened of her entering another world. Jimmy was a council caretaker but had once been a professional soldier. He had survived the trenches of the First World War, bore the unbearable and stood on guard outside Buckingham Palace. A member of the Coldstream Guards, he rose to the rank of Drill Sergeant. He probably felt that she would be outside her comfort zone – who knows! Or that he would lose her to a privileged world.

His mother and father (who was a chimney sweep) were illiterate. His birth certificate has their marks, crosses, not their signatures on them.

Early in my career I ran courses for Drill Sergeants who had developed vocal trauma as they barked across parade grounds. I thought of Jimmy and his voice and world.

My imagination has always pondered that crossroad in Margaret's history. She could have gone to Oxbridge . . .

As it happens, when she met my Dutch father who was in London escaping his own horrors caused by the Second World War – and they were horrors, and in his own way he was cursed – she was rapidly progressing up through the civil service. Making good money and being promoted regularly, she, like most people after the war's death toll, was silently keeping calm and carrying on. Everyone had lost someone. The love of her life was killed in Burma and she lived in quiet, inconsolable grief for the rest of her life. Trevor, her fallen, young love, was in her mind days before her death. His photo clutched in her hand.

And so, she married my father, stopped working and became voiceless.

Turned into an attentive, compassionate listener.

She learnt Dutch effortlessly as she wanted to know what her husband's family was saying, and remained fluent for the rest of her life. Dutch came trippingly off her tongue.

If she was from the middle classes she might have had more muscle and self-esteem to enable her to keep her voice, but she knew her place. Instead, she dealt with her husband's insensitive behaviour and the snobs around her. Margaret, with her flashes of brilliance and sharp observations, rare but potent well-timed barbs. These eloquent phrases could also sting her children: we occasionally received them as a last resort to *our* middle-class arrogance. For women to succeed at that time, they needed enlightened fathers or enlightened husbands. She had neither.

A fine mind and a lost voice: a very common story from women married in the late 1940s and 1950s. Her voice was open and mellow-toned but never loud. Somewhere along her journey, probably at school, she had changed her accent from a Northumberland dialect to neutral standard English. Her grammar was good and her language simple, nothing fussy. But I did hear the power of her voice right at the end.

Mother lay dying in Orpington Hospital just before Christmas 2002.

I slept the nights with her on the floor of her single room. My brother John spent the days with her. She was in and out of consciousness and suffered with dementia.

On the second night she jolted awake and started to cry.

I got into the bed with her and held her. The crying moved into a fully powered wail. She drew the breath in whole and complete and let the cry out full and uninhibited. In the silence of her intake I said, 'You've done a great job, Mum, you've been a wonderful mother.'

Suddenly the wail stopped. Margaret, who hadn't spoken coherently for months, called out, loud and clear. 'It's not enough.'

I held her until she got tired and her distress waned.

'Do you remember, Mum, how you taught me to jump off a swing? At the top of the backward movement of the swing?' I felt her attention gather strength.

She gave the slightest nod and the slightest smile.

Then I said, 'Mum, you can jump now.'

Margaret died the next evening. Christmas night. She was in a foetal position. My brother went to get Father. I shut her eyes. Climbed onto the bed and held her. I spoke poems to her; *Jenny Kiss'd Me*, Sonnets 116 and 18. Then I sang 'Golden Slumbers kiss your eyes, Smiles await you when you rise, sleep darling Mummy, do not cry, And I shall sing a lullaby.'

I noticed that a nurse had come in and was watching me. I felt guilty. I had done something wrong and forbidden. She left without comment. My father arrived and I left Mother with him.

As I walked down the corridor I met the nurse. I thought she would tell me off. I stopped, facing her, expecting the worst.

'I've never seen anyone do what you did . . . ' she said. 'It's the right thing to do.'

I took a breath.

I was eighteen and working in the local library as my nanna lay dying in Farnborough Hospital. Bliss, being around all those books and all those librarians who cared about books. It was my gap year work, and it felt a known place, a safe place. At eight I had found a nearby library, small with only a quiet residential road to be crossed to get there. It was my refuge and joy.

As Nanna was leaving us I would finish work and Margaret and I would visit her. Over the three weeks it took Nanna to pass, we found a ritual.

After the visit, we would go to the local pub for a drink. This was my idea, as Margaret could not believe that a woman without a man could go to a bar and order a drink. It broke all her traditions and female expectations that I could ask for and pay for a drink and some nuts. The first time I did it in her presence her eyes filled with tears of joy. I taught her how to do it and she laughed when she completed her first mission to the bar. Later, when I was working and travelling all over the world, her eyes would fill again as I explained that I could and did sit alone in restaurants. It was hard in the 1980s but I did it and she was so proud of me – and whenever I do it now, her ghost sits with me as I enter the restaurant, sit down, order, eat and pay. It is a delighted ghost.

Nanna was my bardic influence. A working-class storyteller. My nurse from *Romeo and Juliet*. Rude, funny and irreverent.

My mother, who had been evacuated from London to the Sussex countryside and separated from Nanna at thirteen, didn't have a strong relationship with her and had no idea of Nanna's skills in storytelling. Nor had my brother or sister. It was a pleasure reserved for me.

Nanna's gift was her courage and energy when she spoke her stories. A gift that was private, free and eloquent. I knew she had a deep, unshockable place in her, and held secrets.

I am ten and trudging home from school. It is summer and I am puzzling a problem out. *Why are we only allowed to choose a boy to love?* The older girls talked all about boys all the time. *But who says it has to be a boy?* That's the problem. *Aren't you allowed to choose anyone to love?*

I hadn't contemplated sex yet. There was no sex on TV! It was a question of love not sex at that moment. Trudging up the hill, with my boater perched on the back of my head and probably my green blazer buttoned up unevenly, it seemed the most important question in the world.

I knew I had to ask Nanna: she might know. I found her in her room, rocking in her chair, sewing, smoking.

I asked the question.

She stopped rocking and sewing and inhaled deeply. She looked at me fully. Blue, unflinching eyes. Long look, no answer, but a taking-in of me. The slightest nod. She continued rocking, sewing and smoking.

The no answer was rare, if not unique, between us.

So I gathered there was no answer, or that if there was it was an unsure one. What started to gather in my mind was another world, a place in-between sureness. A place that maybe Nanna understood, maybe visited before her late marriage at thirty-eight.

It led me to thinking about otherness.

I didn't feel contempt or disgust or any lack of love from Nanna, just her knowing that she now knew something more of me. She wasn't shocked, but it completed a part of me in her understanding.

Unlike my mother who, at best, when she understood that part of me, felt disappointment and grief, or, at worst, shame, at my uncontainable, unclassifiable passions for both sexes. In today's terms I am fluid – that seems the right word.

In the 1980s, the word was bisexual and it was vilified. Bisexuals were hated by both homosexuals and heterosexuals. They seemed to find the possibility of choice not fair to them. There was the potential of betrayal to both.

I knew as a child that it wasn't about sex or looks. It wasn't about identity, but something else. It was a wholeness, yes, a fluidity and union within the heart and mind. Passion that included emotion and thought. Not one without the other.

Not gender, or beauty, or age. Not the outside of someone but something moving seamlessly inside them – that was what was attractive to me.

Otherness.

An undivided being or one trying to be unboxed, a messy but creative place before containment or commitment.

I found an otherness in Shakespeare. A man who was comfortable with feeling passion for women and men. Addressing sonnets to both. The mind and heart that could flow outside boxes and saw and felt the best and worst in people without flinching.

At least Margaret and Winnifred knew who they were, somehow. My mother learning the rituals to survive, not willingly, but obediently walking into her marriage box.

Nanna never conceding, full of anger and deep scorn for the world.

I began to know they didn't like each other and understood: Nanna had not been an attentive mother.

And me . . . in the middle, sometimes scared that Mummy might be jealous of my love for Nanna and hers for me.

Otherness in love is never simple.

8
WINNIE

In the hospital – dying – she sang. Mostly folk and musical hall songs. And she spoke to the nurses with such kindness and grace that came from her working-class understanding of hard work, saying 'Please' and 'Thank you' to the nurses who lifted and washed her. She encouraged them to sing with her. She was returning to a freedom she hadn't openly shown in my father's house.

The daughter of a station porter in Blythe, Northumberland. Winifred – Winnie to her friends. Nanna to us.

When she was thirteen her schoolteacher approached her father. Winifred was extremely bright and creative. Could he, her teacher, apply to have her trained as a pupil teacher?

Two weeks later her father apprenticed her as a seamstress. She wasn't going to be a teacher. 'Too big for her boots' was the only comment she made about that crossroad and her loss. Presumably, she was quoting her father.

I still have the scissors she was given when she was apprenticed. Rescued from the house clearance of my parent's family home.

Her bedroom was my refuge. Nanna had her dignity and sense of space. I knew it was a privilege to spend time in her smoky, sweet-filled room. Always sweets under the pillow that she sucked on at night when her teeth were out and in the special tooth mug.

Her room was a rationed haven, and because it was rationed I knew it was special and that in her own room she was different.

Her own room.

I can vividly remember sitting there at thirteen. Nanna rocking in her chair, smoking, the ash was on the cigarette. She always caught it in time even when she was sewing. She was a brilliant needlewoman. I suddenly felt her vigorous stare on me. Her fierce spirit reaching out to mine. She stopped rocking, she carefully put the ash into the ashtray. She stopped sewing.

'I hate bloody sewing.'

She made sure she had shocked me. Continued rocking, continued sewing. The shock wasn't meant to be the word 'bloody' – she had a rich and often filthy vocabulary, one that only I heard – I never heard my mother swear. It was the idea that was meant to shock. A shock that took me years to really feel and honour. I knew she had been sewing for sixty years, and I realized in that moment that her life had been spent doing something she hated.

It was the cost I felt years later when I knew that I was spending my life differently. These shocks come more regularly as I leave Winifred and Margaret further behind, and age to meet them.

Leaving Margaret one day after we'd had lunch together in London. 'Where are you going?' she asked.

'To a company called Shared Experience,' I replied. They had a beautiful rehearsal room in Dufour's Place, a converted laundry just around the corner from Silver Place where my mother had lived as a child. I explained where I was going. Margaret, as usual, tried to hide the shock at the coincidence, but said slowly and clearly so that I could understand:

'Nanna used to wash other people's laundry there.'

And so, her ghost, as I worked on great texts upstairs, was scrubbing and wringing out someone else's underwear in the basement.

Nanna's sisters married miners. Her brothers returned from war. Nanna lost the love of her life in the mud of, I believe, The Somme. She talked about him two days before she died. One of her brothers brought Jimmy, my grandfather, home for tea. He had survived the horror. Much younger than Nanna, handsome and always laughing. He had had a spell in the music hall before joining the Coldstream Guards.

It wasn't a happy marriage, though they stayed together.

When my father had to be the one to deliver the news that he had died, she said *I am sorry*. Nothing more. He drank and pawned everything to drink. But then, he had the demons of the trenches.

Nanna resisted him. Refused to go with him when he was stationed outside London, but would go home to Blythe. Refused to bend, and you can see this in her body and spine in the photos of them together.

After leaving the army, Jimmy, now working for the council, got my newly married parents a council flat. Very soon after he died my father came home one day and announced that he had bought the house in the suburbs. He felt obliged to take Nanna with us. There had been no choice but for her to come to live with us after Jimmy, the caretaker, died and she lost their flat.

So my father transplanted Margaret and Winifred who had been living in Pimlico, to a house that needed a long walk to the nearest shop. Mother couldn't drive yet and they were left in a lovely house with a garden, stranded away from their friends, while he pursued his successful career in London, leaving at 7.00 am and returning after 9.00 pm – if he wasn't carousing.

Very occasionally, Nanna would walk to the station and visit a friend in The Smoke. I would meet her off the train if I was out of school. Sometimes she came to meet me from school. It was up to her if we talked on the walk. She had control, but it was a loving one. I would do anything for her. When she couldn't be bothered to make the journey to the shops, she would use me to buy her strong Capstan cigarettes at the local tobacconists, who happily sold them to a schoolgirl.

Nanna stood at my bedroom door every night before I went to sleep to say good night. No kisses or touch – too Northern! But with such care and tenderness. One night I experienced, aged six, the first realization I ever had of death through the knowledge that one day I would suffer the loss of her *good night*. She was old, having had her only child, my mother, at thirty-nine, and I can still feel the terror of knowing she would go. That she would leave me.

Her stories still live in me. Some were fantasies. Others were true. One started:

'There was a girl in our village that messed with pigs. She had a litter, didn't live long . . . '

Or:

'My sister Beatrice always kept a place at the table for her husband. Killed in a mining accident. Never found his body. She was pregnant with her third so I went to stay with her and slept with her in their double bed. One night she woke me and said, turn back the sheet.' In the bed between them lay her newly born son.

The first was fantasy the second the truth – I presume. The fantasy stories – there were many of them – my mother never heard. They were for me.

Then there were the rows. Even as a small child we would row about ideas, fierce and intellectual. About rubbish on the new, colour television. Hard but loving altercations. Again, rows that only I seemed to have with her.

And then there was Shakespeare.

Around the age of nine I requisitioned the battered Shakespeare. I hid it in my room. I was drawn to *Hamlet*, mostly because it started with a ghost.

And because no one told me it was difficult, I seemed to effortlessly understand much of it; and if I didn't understand it, I still enjoyed it. The sounds of the verse, the rhythms, the intriguing puzzle of why it was in verse form or why it suddenly went into prose. I liked it.

I immediately decided it should be shared with Nanna. I think there was also a one-upmanship, as I had found sayings that she had uttered. I was rather pleased with myself that I had found the source.

'The readiness is all.'
'Neither a borrower nor lender be.'
'What a piece of work is a man.'

There were others.

I knocked on her door and was called in. I sat.

She was rocking and sewing. I told her I was reading *Hamlet* by Shakespeare. There was a slight rolling of her eyes. I pronounced that he was very good and clever. More rolling. I had to prove my point and started quoting his lines that I had heard her use. After a while she stopped rocking and sewing. She fixed me with one of her fiercest stares.

'I don't think that's all that clever. We've been saying those things for years.'

I probably had a smug look on my face. I had won. 'You say those things because he wrote them.'

Quick as a whip, Nanna parried: 'He wrote them because we said them.'

At that moment I sensed she was right. Later, I knew that she was. She knew about the attentive listening required of playwrights and the innate articulacy every storyteller has, without any need to be learned or academic.

Shakespeare speaks to us because he heard all who spoke to him, and more importantly, he witnessed it with compassion.

As I grow older I do spend nights trying to remember if I can recall any meaningful exchanges or dialogues Nanna had with my father. I can't.

She lived in his house under his power and his accumulating wealth. I suppose she was frightened of being thrown out.

She did conduct a taste war with him. She knew he found her ritual of boiling her underwear in a special pot on the cooker revolting. She took joy, I am sure, in using her special wooden prodding spoon to stir her knickers around in the bubbling pot when he was in the kitchen and visibly upset.

But in his presence, her voice and articulacy, her humour, her intellect and her fierce rage were closed down.

She kept her rage intact until her death.

As I've said, I was eighteen. My mother was experimenting with her cooking. She went to a weekly cooking class. Nanna didn't approve of the 'foreign stuff' we were suddenly all eating. Nanna's own cooking was dreadful, the only gift was when she made chutney, the rest of her food was to be avoided. My father loved the chutney but was disgusted by the smell it created in the house when she was making it. She had her hidden smile when he complained about the stench, and when he scooped the chutney onto his plate but never with thanks.

Duck a l'orange was the dish. In an act of resistance, Nanna decided to take the duck carcass with meat on it out to the garden to feed the birds. She told me of her intent with a gleam in her eye.

'It's cannibalism!' I exclaimed. 'Birds eating birds!'

She smiled. 'They eat worms and worms are meat.'

'Don't do it, Nanna!' I left for my room. We were the only ones home.

Some time later, I heard her calling. She was in the garden on her back, the duck carcass beside her. She had fallen.

I ran to her.

'Something's happened to me – I heard a crack.'

I ran to phone the ambulance and brought blankets to keep her warm. I sat and held her hand.

'Go get me some whisky!' she said.

I knew she had a small flask of whisky under her bed for the occasional swig.

I don't know how she replenished it – maybe from my father's stock, maybe Mother helped!

'I can't Nanna, they might need to give you drugs.'

'*Get me some whisky.*'

'I can't.'

'Bitch.' Followed by a laugh.

I still experience the shame of my middle class, sensible reaction. That sensible meanness of class. Maybe she was fighting for me not to be tamed.

I went in the ambulance with her and she perked up and flirted with the ambulance man. I had never seen her flirt, clear and charming. Yes, she was right: I didn't know her.

It was her last journey and she was fearless and she was flirting. At eighty-six, free from the middle-class house and her secret dread of being put in a care home, which was what my father was planning.

She died in hospital three weeks later.

My mother wanted to learn and my Nanna wanted to teach.

I wanted to teach because I wanted to learn. You learn very deeply when you teach.

My nanna's lost teaching vocation and Mother's lost education bedded into me and circulated in my blood. It wasn't fair and had to be balanced.

I had to find the doors that had been closed to them by their fathers. Their fathers, who maybe through protection or maybe through envy, had blocked their way. And then their husbands: Nanna resisted hers and Mother didn't.

I know this now, I didn't then; but I did know that if they had been boys their fathers would have burst with pride.

9
MY FATHER

Malcolm   *Dispute it like a man*
Macduff   *I shall do so. But I must also feel it as a man.*

My father, Max, was a gentleman.

He had impeccable manners and entertained generously and lavishly. He loved a good party. He laughed a lot in public. He was a hard worker and had loyal and loving male friends. When it was required, this good-looking man was charming and attentive.

He started as an office boy in a publishing company and worked his way up to run the company. He helped to sponsor the Abortion Act, the Clean Air Act and the cleaning of the Thames. He never lost his Dutch accent and his English was sometimes hesitant. He believed correctly that this worked to his advantage in the English class system: nobody could tell where he fitted into it.

At his funeral there were people I didn't know who loved him. He had his work world and his family world.

Max drank.

In the 1980s, I was teaching alongside the great violinist and conductor Yehudi Menuhin. With me was a composer whose parents had been in Auschwitz.

A group of us had lunch with Yehudi. I remember he listened to us all intently. At one point he turned to the composer and said, 'You have been touched by the curse of Nazism.'

It was so simply spoken that there was no shock but the truth. The meal continued and as it finished and I was standing to leave the table to teach, Yehudi looked at me: 'And you too have been touched by the curse.' In that moment he had handed me a piece of the secret that had been standing in plain sight all my life. My father.

And these pieces were well hidden in a family that wasn't present with each other. They have had to be pushed and dragged into the light. I still only know bits.

The movie in my head can see the sixteen-year-old Max on 10 May 1940, watching the paratroopers of the Third Reich drifting down on parachutes into his country, The Netherlands. I don't know whether it was his idea, but he ran to the town hall to help destroy papers, including names and addresses of the whole population. An extremely astute first action of resistance. Knowledge, for the Nazis, was power. Max's act took some of that knowledge from them.

I can barely imagine what my father saw, did and felt during the war, but I know that it was terrible. This *is* a curse. Max hid enormous violence and the drink unusually dulled it. That and the loud playing of jazz: Duke Ellington and Ella Fitzgerald.

I gathered bits of his story, over many years, in isolated moments of revelation.

I found out as a teenager that he had helped take part in the brutal ritual, happening all over liberated Europe – shaving the heads of women who had collaborated in his home town – he felt, once again, my rage at him. He didn't take the bait, but merely said, 'They ate with the Gestapo while we starved.' Holland did starve in early 1945. The Battle of The Bulge was raging and their liberators couldn't get to them quickly enough. That freezing winter, Max lived off tulip bulbs.

Later, I learned that his girlfriend had had her legs blown off, and that he had pushed her in a wheelbarrow, trying to find help. She died in the wheelbarrow. This revealed, again, in an almost casual once-off remark.

Then he spoke simply, once, of being forced to dig his own grave at twenty-one and managing to escape, running desperately, when a spitfire appeared. His only remark when I questioned him about this extraordinary piece of information, which he had uncharacteristically let slip, was, 'If you're being shot at, run in a zig-zag.' And that's all I ever learned about that momentous moment of survival.

Almost the last thing he said as he struggled to die was: 'I never forgave my father for not resisting.' Another vital piece of his story, left hanging with no explanation.

At Max's funeral I spoke Shakespeare's words from *Henry V* before the battle of Agincourt.

And gentlemen in England now a-bed
Shall think themselves accursed they were not here,
And hold their manhoods cheap whiles any speaks
That fought with us upon Saint Crispin's day

It was my understanding of how my father was tested and stood his ground, and fought the fear to do what was right, that enabled me to forgive him. The violence and the fear of a young man in the wrong moment of history.

And he needed forgiving.

Resistance

It was hard to talk to my father about things that really mattered to me. Those who hold the power in any relationship can choose not to speak about subjects that they find uncomfortable. Max never tolerated subjects he didn't want to hear, so you either had to trick him into a conversation you wanted, or raise your voice and push him into it.

I always had to make an appointment to speak with him. It had to be on his terms, in his house and lounge – a place my mother eventually avoided. A sickness would gather in my stomach and I would practise the content as I would practise my lesson plans.

I was frightened.

'Is this a good time to speak about . . . ?'

Grunt.

If he wasn't already reading the *Financial Times* he would pick it up, open it, and either read or pretend to read.

Some meetings would end without any contribution from him, maybe a twitching of the paper. Had anything been heard? What were his thoughts?

As a child, I decided to stand my ground and not tolerate how he treated my mother or Nanna.

Like many fathers in the 1950s he wasn't interested in children and being ignored is not good for a child. I also knew that what little attention I received from him was the wrong kind.

He would compete with me in strange and hurtful ways, and these actions were supposed to be a joke; if I didn't laugh, it proved in his mind that I was an unpleasant, unlikeable, unjoyful child.

My Dutch Oma, my father's mother, was visiting. The whole family was walking in Kelsey Park. I was five. I had been given my sister's hand-me-down tricycle, which I found enormous joy in riding. I was zipping backwards and forwards on the bike, looping around the walking group. My father had his rolled-up businessman's umbrella with him. He started to try and catch the bike as I passed with his umbrella handle. He was aiming to stop me by hooking the bicycle under the seat. The first time he managed it I was jerked off the bike and scraped my knees in the fall.

He laughed.

I was furious. I wasn't going to be de-railed in this way, so began the loop again but faster, to outsmart him.

What I remember next was a moment I learnt to identify as the turning point from a game into something much darker. He was getting determined to remove me from the bike and with this determination came his fury.

I continued, though I understood that the game was now different. I then heard Oma speaking with her son in Dutch. She was angry with him. I heard my name and knew she was defending me. Oma, a frightening, matriarchal figure, who, with her sisters, *did* resist – one great aunt forged papers for downed RAF airmen. From Oma I did sense a hard and puritan approval, but I never got to know her well.

My father stopped the attack on me and my bike: Oma was the first person who I could feel witnessing what he was doing to me. She helped me to feel that I had won and that it, and he, were worth resisting.

As my father's career took off he wasn't around much, but when he was it could be a harsh and sometimes physical experience. Some years ago I realized I had a fear of walking upstairs in front of people; I had to let them go before me. The memories came back immediately. Only one room in the house had a lock – the bathroom. I learnt that if one of my well-timed barbs to him hit home, I needed to run up the stairs to the bathroom and lock myself in until he calmed down. I didn't always make it. His technique was to chase and grasp my legs and pull them from under me.

The punishment was fast and physical.

My clearest memory is of the eight-year-old me challenging his knowledge of music. He had a boxed set of *Reader's Digest* records. I played them constantly. I believed they were mine, as he rarely seemed interested in classical music. One evening he was searching through the set and chose a record and placed it on the stereo record player. I had put the record in the wrong sleeve: Mozart in a Wagner sleeve. He settled back with his whisky to listen.

'I like Wagner. Very good.' A contented remark, a sigh and a sip of his favourite drink.

The words bubbled into my mouth.

'You don't know much if you think Mozart is Wagner.'

I again identified the turning point.

The glass was put down, the rage that indicated that I had finally got his attention focused in his eyes and the chase began.

My mother was powerless to stop him or me.

After he had hurt me and I had gone into self-isolation in my room, lying straight and rigid with rage on my bed, he would come up and sit on the bed to say sorry. He would pat me on the shoulder and I would not utter a sound. I would not accept his apology. I would not come down for supper. I was more stubborn than he was. In this way I thought I had won the round.

Nanna would come up, after supper, with a plate of my favourite food that she had gathered. An act of kindness but also one of solidarity.

She wouldn't say much, but would put the plate down, nod and leave.

There was a routine my father did for a period of time when I was around eleven. He performed this routine like a music-hall act.

'*You can't have your cake and eat it*,' he would say.

Pause.

'I don't understand this saying, It's stupid. I can have a cake and eat it and then buy another cake.'

After the first time this pronouncement was made he knew it was going to upset me.

'No, you can't.'

'Yes, I can.'

'If you eat the cake it won't be there.'

'I can buy another cake.'

'But that's not the saying. It's a cake. There is no "s" on the word. It's not *cakes*. It is one cake.'

This normally ended with me shrieking in that high vocal tone designed to be so unpleasant that the listener gives in to shut you up.

My father never conceded this one. Many wealthy, white men, powerful and handsome, have through millennia figured out that they could have a cake and buy another one.

After my mother died, his PA for more than forty years became very prominent in his life.

We gradually realized that our father was the love of her life, and she now had full access to him. She quickly became a constant in the family home. It was agreed that I should investigate, particularly when she started to throw our mother's belongings out of the house. The usual fear began to build in my body and breath as I prepared to talk to him.

'Is Clare in love with you?'

That familiar smirk of '*Of course*. Yes.'

'Did Mum know?'

'Oh no. I loved your mother!'

'But Clare has adored you for forty years.'

'Yes. Loves me.'

'So you would go to work from a house with a woman you loved, to work, where there was another woman who loved you.'

'Yes.'

'Did she go out drinking with you?'

'Of course. With all the other men. We all thought it was funny, her tagging along.'

He laughed.

'So you did have your cake and ate it.'

He started to laugh again. Stopped. Glared. Got up and refilled his gin and tonic.

My father constantly tested me and I tested him, and it was hard but necessary. At the time, I didn't realize that it was the only way to maintain a fragment of my voice. But it was. And I learnt a lot.

I was in my forties the last time I opened an important issue with my father, the newspaper blocking his face from my view. I gave up trying to engage him. My voice louder than usual:

'Have you ever wondered why I have dedicated my life to voice and presence?'

The paper twitched and I allowed the pause to hold, the silence to stay.

The paper came down and we made eye contact. There was a small nod and I do believe there was a shift. He never used the newspaper as a shield again.

At his grand retirement party from the publishing company, I was at a far-flung table sitting next to a journalist I had never met. At a moment in my father's speech, after he had once again glanced my way, this journalist whispered to me, 'I have often wondered who your father was frightened of . . . Now I know: it's you.'

I never knew whether this was a compliment or a criticism, but the shock was cellular. What a cost, a price to keep my voice and not concede.

The loss and the gain.

My father had hurt me; and at that moment, I realized that my presence and resistance had hurt him. So much of my youthful energy had been focused on defending myself and my mother and Nanna.

It had never occurred to me that it might have had an effect on him.

Drowning

The violence did stop after an event when I was eleven. And although this particular incident was always on the surface of my memory, I had to suffer a three-day struggle with breathing, twenty-seven years later at the age of thirty-eight – a serious attack of late-onset asthma in my farmhouse in Portugal – before it came into acute focus as an embodied memory.

The trigger for this episode in my adulthood was a cat: I started to suffer a powerful attack on my breath system. I know that I only survived because I knew how to breathe. I had no telephone and anyway, at that time the Portuguese Ambulance Service was rudimentary. I knew I had to breathe through and decide to live. As night came, the house seemed to fill with ghosts watching askance as I fought to breathe in and then, most importantly, fully breathe out.

Ghosts of those, some still alive, who had tried to stop me breathing. Then, appearing on my shoulders, the imprint of my father's bare feet.

In the summer of 1965 when I was eleven, we were on holiday in Apeldoorn, my father's home town in the Netherlands. The real joy for me in that visit was that there was a magnificent, open-air swimming pool, and swimming is one of the loves of my life. I am a strong swimmer.

My father was a champion swimmer and played water polo before the war. He was good enough for his friends to still comment on his past triumphs many years later. We children spent days at the pool with my mother. One day we were joined by Max, who swam impressively, length after length. I kept up with him rather well, and then what I thought was a game commenced. He ducked me. There was laughter. He ducked me again and laughed and turned to swim away.

I saw his back, climbed on it and ducked him, laughing.

I was enjoying the fact that I'd got him under when he surfaced, flicking the hair out of his eyes, and faced me. I saw the turning point. It was no longer a game and I couldn't swim away.

Furious, he ducked me. I had air and went under. I came up and gasped. I got some air but not enough. He ducked me again. I came up and couldn't get enough air before he ducked me. Next time up was shouting for him to stop. He ducked me. I had very little air. I came up. I couldn't get air. I was ducked again. We were in the deep end and this time he put his feet on my shoulders and pushed down to hold me on the bottom of the pool. In the watery distance I could hear my mother shouting. I couldn't hear words but I could hear her voice. I felt the bottom of the pool with my feet and saw his feet on my shoulders.

And then a calm came over me and I felt my ribcage shrink and begin to set me free.

Suddenly he was dragging me up. Pulling me, gasping, to the side of the pool. I clung on to the bar that ran along the side, wheezing, crying.

He swam off and continued doing his lengths.

My mother was there with a towel and the event was over. Not talked about, not even allowed to hang in the air.

Twenty-seven years later, back in the farmhouse, I breathed and breathed until the imprint of his feet faded. How interesting that so many ghosts crowded around me then and even now there are people I have loved that I feel try to drown me.

Drown thyself! drown cats and blind puppies.

                                                                    Iago, *Othello*

This line flew out from the page in my early reading of *Othello*. And it was obvious to my young mind that Othello needed to suffocate Desdemona, stopping her breath, not stabbing her.

A year after my asthma attack I was sitting in the farmhouse with Mother. She loved Portugal and we would go together, without my father, which he thought was unfair.

I asked her about the unspoken event.

She was calm and relieved.

'Did it happen?' I said.

'Yes it happened.'

'You were shouting for him to stop?'

'Yes.'

I could feel her shame and her helplessness. We stood up together and held a long hug.

Then she said, 'He never hit you again. He knew he could've drowned you.'

After Mother had died I asked him the same question. He laughed. 'It was a game!' And then after the shortest pause. 'I beat you.'

'I was eleven and you had your feet on my shoulders.'

'That is how we do it in water polo.' He stood up to refresh the scotch. 'But you didn't drown. You survived.'

My father's violence stopped, but my resistance couldn't. Especially when I was fuelled up by the wave of feminism in the early 1970s, reading and listening to brilliant female thinkers.

I remember a heated debate with him when I spoke about Virginia Woolf's *A Room of One's Own*. The simple concept of a woman having her own room was a physical insult and a rejection of his body. 'Why would a wife sleep anywhere else but beside her husband?'

If I won a point then he would grunt and get up to freshen his whisky. My mother would sit silently but attentively, hiding a smile and thrilled with the idea of her own room. My father was a champion snorer.

The bond with my mother deepened in this alliance against him.

This hurt him, as I would deliberately defend her and devise strategies to wound him when he was careless and cruel to her.

In my thirties I was having a drink with a company of actors in a South London pub. It was a Friday, an early evening in June.

It was only after ten minutes that I realized, to my shame and shock, that sitting at the bar with a whisky was my father, flirting with the barmaid. She obviously knew him.

He didn't see me. My heart bled for my mother waiting in the suburbs on her own. I excused myself and managed to escape unseen by him.

I drove to their home. I found my mother, packed a weekend bag for her and drove her down to Eastbourne. We checked in to the Grand Hotel and ordered room service.

Later, when I knew my father would be back, I phoned and said we were having a weekend by the sea.

My mother loved the sea. Her greatest joy was walking on the beach. We had a grand weekend and when I took her back he was very upset. He expressed abandonment. He never hurt her physically, but he ignored her to the point of abuse. Max loved Margaret and I don't think he ever believed his behaviour was a constant abandonment of her.

After this, I discovered several of his drinking pit stops on his journey home. He didn't want to go home. Work, his colleagues, were fun. Children and marriage were not.

It's true that he never hit me again, but he found other ways to hurt me.

The lesser way was never to praise any of my achievements, although I knew by some of his behaviour that I had passed his approval rating. He loved and owned beautiful cars and I was allowed to drive them – no one else was.

I won sporting events, poetry speaking competitions, scholarships, awards. I wrote books – and there were no positive comments, only negative. I stopped expecting.

A few years before his death, a close friend sat with him at a party, and across the room I heard her tell him how professional and respected I was. His response: 'I don't care about anything she does.'

As I see it, there are three attacks that men can easily make on a woman's presence, power and voice. Attacks that can freeze our ability to have any self-worth or belief in anything we are or do.

Our looks and/or lack of beauty or attractiveness; our lack of humour or inability to smile at them or laugh at their unfunny jokes; and probably – at the root of it all – our unlikability. If we women are not liked we are at risk and vulnerable.

My father had a routine when introducing my elder sister and I.

Indicating my sister: 'This is the beautiful one.'

Then me: 'This is the clever one. Chalk and cheese.'

He always expected a laugh at this observation. I didn't laugh at his jokes, particularly when I realized they were mocking me – he wanted me to laugh at the wounds he inflicted. It was a double win if I were to laugh.

I grant I was a serious child. A deep thinker. I understood that my father's 'jokes' aimed at me were not funny but mocking, and I was expected to laugh at these words that were reducing me. Maybe it is the way men banter together – and maybe if I could have bantered back I would be allowed to join the 'club'. But I was a child and the jokes hurt. They were not the quality of jokes my brother and sister received. They were jokes about things I couldn't do, mistakes I made, things I had achieved, my body, my thoughts.

When I was thirteen, I read with great excitement that Tchaikovsky's *1812 Overture* – complete with canons – was being performed at Croydon's Fairfield Halls. I went to my mother: 'May I go?'

She was not a music fan. I couldn't go on my own. 'Ask your father.'

As usual, I was nervous. I waited until they were both together. I showed him the advert in the local paper. He addressed my mother.

'I don't want to be seen with her, she's ugly.'

I don't remember any pain at the time.

Maybe I knew already; maybe I knew he had been drinking; maybe I just wanted to go, and his response made my mother agree to take me.

My rage only came across years later as I looked at photos of myself. It wasn't true. It was a lie. I didn't try to make myself attractive, but it wasn't true.

Even to the end of his life he would send a flowery birthday card to my sister and one with a pig on it to me. Eventually my father understood I wasn't laughing, which triggered the next pronouncement: 'Patsy has no sense of humour.'

I believed I had no sense of humour until I was in my twenties. Then I found I could make the people I taught laugh, and the laughter was shared and pure and fun. No agenda, just enjoyment in the room.

Being liked

Many women carry the relentless need for, and pursuit of, being liked. Of course, some men pursue this too, but usually not so desperately. Realistically, you cannot make people like you. It's not in your control. We seek the impossible, and by doing so generally make ourselves less liked!

I teach women that, in formal leadership roles, it's not ethical to seek being liked. Yes, seek fairness, balance and a good use of power; but all these positive things are warped by trying to be liked. The duplicitous will use it against you, the honourable will not feel safe.

I am not saying you won't be liked – it is the *need* to be liked that is so destructive. And women in power generally have to work hard against this need.

I always knew my father didn't like me.

He definitely knew I wasn't impressed, as most people were, with him. But I accepted his dislike and indifference towards me very early in life. I chose at that time to do nothing about it.

Then in my mid-thirties, an event that was so shocking, but so freeing, occurred. A revelation that was such a relief and such a sharpening of perspective that it helped me on my journey through the male world which I, like all women, have had to push through. A barbed-wire gift that transformed me and, set me free.

My sister Susan suffered severe brain damage a few days after giving birth to her second child.

She was in the Hospital for Nervous Diseases, as it was then known, in Queen's Square. Overnight, she was disabled. Every day at lunch time I would go to reteach her to speak. Every evening my father would visit her.

At the time I had a house in Camberwell and, if he saw I was home, he used my house as another drinking pit stop.

One evening I was entertaining. My dearest friend Kelly McEvenue was staying. I was cooking in the basement kitchen and Father arrived. Once again, he had been drinking. He loved Kelly and enjoyed her company. He came down and continued on my red wine.

We began talking about Susan. Before long, he became maudlin and sentimental. How her brain had been destroyed, how bad it was.

I was chopping salad, my back to him.

Then he said, 'Poor Susie, poor, poor Susie.' There was a pause. I felt his eyes fixed on my back. I put down the knife, I turned to face him. He looked me straight in the eyes, clear and direct.

'I wish it had been you.'

There it was. Words out of his mouth. Existing, being there. The truth. What I had always known.

Now, Kelly is a brilliant Alexander Technique teacher, so can handle bodies. Before I could take a breath she was on her feet, carefully taking his glass out of his hand.

'You don't speak to Patsy like that, in her own house, drinking her wine!' She had him on his feet, pushed him up the stairs and wrenched open the front door. I walked to the basement window and watched as dear Kelly ejected him onto the street.

So here was the question: why did he seek my company? And the answer came as clearly as the knowledge of his dislike.

He loved me.

Death

My father suffered a massive stroke in November 2015, aged eighty-seven. It was a Friday and he was unconscious when I got down to the house. We all gathered. I slept beside him that night.

In the morning he came to. I was there. He was looking around and suddenly became very present and then looked at me unmasked, true and clear.

And as clearly as he ever spoke.

'Oh Patsy, you're here.'

There it was. The love.

That Saturday afternoon at 1.00 pm he suffered another massive stroke, which both my brother and I witnessed.

He went into a coma and died three days later.

In his life, Max had had no skills to deal with me. I wasn't compliant.

And he was a creature of his time. He was careless and cruel to his wife and family. He drank with journalists who openly groped women and told filthy jokes in our presence. Rape jokes. 'Slut' jokes. He didn't have to budge, as his actions were not challenged. Max had no reason to change, no voices except mine demanding his change, and therefore he had no strategies to be a better husband or father.

His male mentors were heavy drinking, heavy smoking, well-educated, promiscuous journalists. All war weary, all survivors that had no reason to work on any of their behaviours. They drove their cars and sloshed and laughed when they smashed them. One of his best friends stole a bulldozer while drunk and drove it up the then-unbarricaded

Downing Street and parked it outside Number 10. He was told off and sent home.

And I now understand, fundamentally, that the war and its violence gave him post-traumatic stress disorder (PTSD), which wasn't recognized or understood in his lifetime. Beyond the trauma, his peers were grown men deprived of their adolescence by war, making up for it, forgetting what they'd been through, and no one said that they should be home with their family. They were having a ball. The seventies slammed into them and they kicked back.

In my late teens, when I started investigating the history of female oppression, I came to recognize how hard it could be, from the male point of view, to transform. I understood that if *I* had had that power for thousands of years, it would be extremely difficult to give up.

Particularly if this power was endorsed in religious texts and secular laws that freely allow men to harm women without retribution.

The gift my father gave me was never to turn me against men. Rather, it was an ability, at a very young age, to recognize behaviours and patterns that I came to realize, as I entered the adult world, are predominantly male. Habits which, because of their unchallenged power through the ages, have become accepted, by both men and women as the right way to behave.

I can't deny that my father loved me.

I coach many actors in playing Goneril in *King Lear*. She is not Lear's favourite – Cordelia is. Lear is in Goneril's palace behaving appallingly – trashing the place. Striking her gentleman.

> *By day and night he wrongs me. Every hour*
> *He flashes into one gross crime or other*
> *That sets us all at odds. I'll not endure it.*

Most actors default to generalized anger, playing Goneril as some distorted, evil woman.

But it's more complex. A father wronging you is hard because it's to do with love.

The moment you say, 'I'll not endure it,' is the moment of liberation.

So many people who knew my father thought him a remarkable man – and he was. I confused him. I loved him but would not be seen as unequal. I didn't have to make the decision 'not to endure it'. It was just there.

The perspective of time makes me kinder to him, particularly when I have male colleagues and clients my age or younger who are still behaving badly towards women. Still kissing students on the mouth, still hugging them too close, slapping their bottoms, looking at their breasts instead of their eyes. Shocked when women take them on, shocked when they don't flirt back or laugh at their jokes, shocked that their power is challenged.

Sonnet 94
They that have power to hurt and will do none,
That do not do the thing they most do show,
Who, moving others, are themselves as stone,
Unmoved, cold, and to temptation slow:
They rightly do inherit heaven's graces
And husband nature's riches from expense;
They are the lords and owners of their faces,
Others but stewards of their excellence.
The summer's flower is to the summer sweet
Though to itself it only live and die,
But if that flower with base infection meet,
The basest weed outbraves his dignity:
For sweetest things turn sourest by their deeds;
Lilies that fester smell far worse than weeds.

10
EDUCATION

I realize now, as I grow older, that my vocation was made inevitable through brief and fully present encounters. Like small pieces of coloured glass that form a stained glass window, only coming together with distance and time.

I remember weeping alone in the stalls of Greenwich Theatre watching the last scene of *The Glass Menagerie* by Tennessee Williams. In the last speech, the main character, Tom, has run away from his mother and sister. His disabled sister collects glass animals and wherever he runs to she haunts him through the coloured glass bottles in shop windows. I could not understand logically how I understood the grief in Tom, but that is the magic of theatre. We understand things before they happen to us, or they are locked away so deeply that a man speaking exact poetic images summons the memory of a similar exactness out of us.

I was alone in the theatre because my family didn't have any desire to go with me. And even the memory of being alone in the theatre at sixteen is shocking to realize now, as my career has made it very necessary to sit alone, at the back of the theatre – the worst seats for audibility in the house – for forty-five years on and off!

I always knew my real quest was communication and presence. And yet, this vocation has shame attached to it for me, as I have always found speaking and being present difficult. The wound is deep and I still find it raw to the touch. I teach what I find difficult to do. The quest has been not to produce beautiful, upper-class speaking, but to re-empower the voice in those who are unable to release their own, their words and ideas. How to refind the natural magnificence of every voice. And, of course, women have been central in this quest, because they are at the bottom of the heap in most people's thinking, and still have to *choose* to speak out, have an opinion and express it with ease, which is the deepest quality in any authoritative action.

As a child who was a shy and reluctant conversationalist, being sent to elocution didn't improve me, but it did make me intrigued as to why I wasn't improving. I knew I had a voice, but it wouldn't obey me. My voice wasn't released or placed, so exercises on speech and range didn't work.

If exercises don't work and shift you then why work on them? This resulted in my teacher reporting me as being lazy!

My passions at school were poetry, Shakespeare, philosophy, English literature and history. By the time I was thirteen I found my way to the theatre, which I would visit as much as I could.

At first, aged thirteen, I went to The New Theatre Bromley, and then I began to travel to the Greenwich Theatre or The Old Vic in London. Now I know that great acting kept me present in a way that wasn't possible at home.

I didn't know I was searching for voice and vocal empowerment, but I did realize that I was searching for important stories, truthful speaking and an engaged storyteller.

I yearned for dialogue and debate.

When I was five, I was sent to a small, mixed school where I stayed until I was nine. Miss Otway, who owned the school, was an eccentric, brilliant woman; she taught seven-year-olds Socrates debate.

Miss Otway also made us learn a poem each week, and if we didn't learn it accurately, we had to stay behind until we did.

What I enjoyed studying was not the voice, but the words and the structures. What I understood, very early, thanks to Mother's love of poetry and Nanna's storytelling, was that thought, rhythm, pace and the sound and sense of words, only revealed themselves to me as I spoke them aloud or heard them.

Eventually, I began to take part in drama, and a singing teacher taught us a singer's classical breath system.

In an all girls' school I got to play lead Shakespeare roles. Our voice direction consisted of the head teacher ringing a handbell at the back of the hall if she couldn't hear us – even with an audience. This might sound extreme, but it was no different than in the theatre, when members of the audience would call out if they couldn't hear. This was a regular occurrence. The audience demanding the whole story. Now it is rare, and it's sad that the audience has been tamed so that they don't demand a fully audible story.

Most of my teachers would not be allowed to teach today; they were either not qualified or were too eccentric. They wandered off the curriculum, and inspired us with unorthodox flashes of passion and sometimes harsh truths.

But, at the age of fifteen, I started to read books which, if I mentioned them to my teachers, were either dismissed or seemed to trouble them.

Then there was my Latin teacher who noticed what I was reading and seeking, Mrs Breakey. She slipped me, I now know at some risk to herself, a copy of Plato's *Symposium*.

The great Greek debate on love. *The Symposium* was interesting and very intellectually engaging, but I was puzzled as there was no mention of women. When I mentioned that to Mrs Breakey she roared with laughter and satisfaction. I had found another piece of the puzzle. The great Greek discussion on love never mentions women.

I still have a Greek drama book that my drama teacher gave me to read. I failed to return it as it was so exciting. It was newly bought, so I should have known that she needed it back. The book was published in 1968 and contained a selection of Greek plays. The translation was literal, academic and hard to decipher, but I was hooked.

I had learnt Latin but not Greek. In order to decipher these plays, I had to search the library and send many sighing librarians to retrieve books from reserve stock. I was piecing a puzzle together, and the real shock came when I read Aeschylus's *The Eumenides*. The Furies, the women, the crones, the ugly ones, the fearful ones. The ones who chased and haunted men who had wronged women and children, and sought justice for them.

The Furies pursuing Orestes who murdered his mother for killing his father, the great warrior and conqueror of Troy, Agamemnon. But Agamemnon had sacrificed his daughter to change the wind, to sail to Troy. A mother was killing the killer of her daughter. I can understand that, I thought. Male violence started the killing spree. A father wrongly killing his daughter and calling it a sacrifice. Why do we all have to be sacrificed? But how comforting I found it that there were a group of women chasing men.

I liked these Furies.

I liked the theatrical coup Aeschylus produced in *The Eumenides*. The Furies were not supposed to be seen. Their horror was not to be shown. So he put them on stage. I was delighted to discover that the shock of ugly, powerful women on stage had such an effect that men fainted.

I had also found out that women were not in the audience in Ancient Greece. These great plays of power, leadership and moral debate were only heard by men. There were a few women prostitutes allowed to attend, the aptly named 'flute girls', the women servicing male erections.

I needed to discuss *The Eumenides* with someone. My mother found these texts too raw, and I knew she would not approve of the Furies – mostly because they lacked feminine appeal. She had already made it very clear to me that the way I dressed and argued and didn't want my hair permed into an unmovable mass was not a productive way to work in the world.

Even as a four year old I would struggle and fight her when she tried to put a pretty dress on me.

She gave up, but couldn't resist the occasional barb about my clothes, weight and hair.

She believed in trying your best. Trying to make a good impression – like my sister. Perfectly coiffured and dressed, nails polished – she had 'successful' boyfriends.

Later my mother recognized the error of her ways.

For some forgotten reason I took her to see Deborah Warner's 1987 production of *Titus Andronicus* in the Barbican Pit. I had done work on the show. Lavinia watches her husband being murdered. She is raped by the two killers, her hands chopped off and her tongue cut out to stop her from naming the offenders.

Lavinia, in that production, appeared with her atrocious mutilations, blood and filth all over her clothes, and kept the same dress on until the end of the play and her death.

At the end of the show, over a glass of wine, my mother's only comment was, 'Why didn't they clean her up and put a new dress on her?'

'Mum, so a newly ironed dress, a bath and maybe bows around her stumps would make it alright?'

She looked at me and started to laugh until the tears rolled down her face. We laughed together. She paused after she recovered, and through the power of theatre she made a crucial connection.

A few years earlier my sister had suffered her devastating brain haemorrhage. As we visited her in Queen's Square Hospital it was painfully apparent that her husband and her friends didn't visit her. This beautiful and well-turned out woman had been abandoned. That night in the theatre, Mum looked me in the eyes: 'When Susan was in the hospital and she didn't have visitors, I thought, Patsy would have visitors. Patsy has loyal friends.'

'So my hair and clothes are not that important?' I teased.

'Yes,' she agreed. 'It's the outside, not you, not your inside – but you could have both.' She always in a quiet and unassuming way got the last comment in!

When I was fifteen and first discovered them, I went to Nanna to talk about *The Eumenides*, the rage, the fury.

She smoked and sucked her mint simultaneously – a habit that always intrigued me.

She wasn't impressed. 'Why are you telling me? Because I'm old and ugly and angry? A hag?'

'No, I think they're interesting.'

Long pause. Sucking noises, the saliva moving around her dentures.

'Maybe they're not all old and ugly, maybe some of them are young and beautiful.'

'Nanna, the plays say they are old and ugly.'

'That's a man saying that. Maybe when women show their rage the men see age and ugliness. Many women are hit for their rage and hit more because they are young and beautiful. Men see what they want to see.'

The rage of *The Eumenides* pleased me even more after that. Nanna could be right.

I knew it was a feeling I wasn't allowed to show without being punished for it. *Were women allowed rage?* I thought I knew that rage was held deep in my body and breath. Sitting there, deep and not allowed. Not womanly. Woman, womb. I can remember the tree I was looking at when those words married each other and became one idea. That is where our power lives. In the womb, giving birth, creating, but also where the deep breath needs to reach into, releasing the muscles, so we can find our full voice and rage and right to speak. Down in the underworld. The womb of the earth.

I was upset that Athene the Goddess of wisdom appeased the Furies, renamed them 'The Kind Ones' (kind – that was what my Mother asked me to be when I argued with my father. 'Be kind to him.') and sent them away from daylight and human sight into the womb, down through a cave into the earth. The reverse of the birth channel, going back into the womb.

I thought these Greek, male writers knew something very important about women's power. There were clues everywhere.

Our rage disgusts men and must be tamed. It reminds them of our power and their injustice towards us.

Debate, theatre, music, architecture, maths, the psyche through verbal expression. Metaphor. The balance between reason and feeling. All this came through the Greeks and was then refound, reborn into Europe through the Renaissance.

But the legacy for women was devastating.

The Greeks conducted a strategic campaign to destroy all the matriarchal societies their navy could physically reach. They shut women away behind closed doors: their purpose in life was to have children and weave. *Because* of the power of women's voices, not because of their powerlessness.

The Greeks had a conscious knowledge and a frightening memory of women's power. A warning that prompted the genocide of women. Women feature in the plays – that no women saw – as a terrifying energy when unleashed, a power that was fearful and unstoppable. And with fear comes hate. So women could not be allowed their rightful equality, the share of the world they were due: not just their empathy and childbearing, but their brilliant minds, their strength, their creativity, and yes, their rational thinking.

The Furies came to me daily in my early womanhood before 1975. Their rage locked in the lower breath of most women that I knew, and some men. In the 1970s, sitting discussing ideas with other women was dangerous. We were not casing the joint for men, reacting with pleasure at their comments and offers of drinks, or inviting them to join the group, we were often treated as Furies.

First approach – 'Hello ladies, need some company?'

Our polite response – 'No, thank you.'

Second approach – 'Oh, you don't want to be sitting there all alone!'

Our firmer response – 'We're not alone.'

First hit – 'What's your problem?'

Second hit – 'You're ugly anyway.'

Third hit – 'Knew it – hairy lesbians.'

Fourth hit – 'What you girls need is a good seeing to, but you're not worth raping.'

This exchange may seem hard to believe now, but any women sitting engrossed in conversation without any men present at that time could quote this scene to you verbatim. Leaving pubs was a survival technique.

When I was at school, the other girls learned about the Furies, but they weren't interested. They were interested in boys and being popular. I was thought too serious by the girls and all the boys I met, and when I went out on a few dates I had to hold my power with boys as I had had to do with my father.

The choice was clear and the sacrifice immediate. I dated a beautiful, intelligent young man a year older than me.

I liked him.

It was summer and he suggested we had a game of tennis.

I was a good – no, a very good player. I had won tournaments and was coached by top coaches. He didn't know this. I tried to avoid playing, but he insisted. He said he loved the game.

We got to the court and began to warm up. I saw the first flicker of surprise on his face as I returned the ball with pace and precision. As we warmed up our serves, my heavy spin serve produced more than surprise on his face – horror began to grow.

He won the toss and served. I won the game.

As we changed sides and crossed over, his eyes dared me to win and they also showed me the consequences of winning.

As I bounced the ball to prepare for my serve – I can still see the ball bouncing by my foot, the plimsoll I was wearing – I watched the bounce and a clear voice in my head said, 'You can win the game and lose him or lose the game and lose yourself.'

I looked up and saw him ready to receive the serve.

I served.

He barely won a point in the two sets we played. I never saw him again.

Ask any woman, and she will have had a similar experience. A story which is about a moment when you don't deny your power, intelligence, wit or talent, knowing that you risk the loss of someone you care about. I was lucky that it happened so young in my life. Many women are much older when they have to stand by their power, and the loss is much harsher. I wasn't in love with him, so the stakes weren't that high.

A whole me would have challenged my husband about his drinking before I married him. I couldn't imagine my life without him, yet somehow knew that he would choose the booze. I was too scared to test him. Like many who love, I believed my feelings for him would defeat and replace the alcohol. Maybe my mother thought the same of my father. But love has to be tested, and we can only test those we love if we have enough self-esteem, if we have equality and are therefore not frightened.

Shakespeare's plays test love. Sometimes the girl has to be in disguise as a man for her potential husband to be able to hear her intelligence and therefore hear her equality and her gravitas.

As I got older, some women and men knew my seriousness was useful.

Sometimes strangers would see my seriousness and trust me. I started to hear confessions.

At seventeen I began to work in a large department store. I was doing two gap years. I was quickly promoted and was running a toy department. Working under me was a woman in her late forties. Beautifully dressed, coiffured, manicured, she made it very clear that her day off was Wednesday. No arguments.

She was a proud and impressive woman. We started to talk. She was smart and handsome. Not married. This was a no-go subject that I honoured. It didn't seem like she had many friends: A loner. Not educated but well read. We talked books and ideas. Then one day, when no one was in the shop, I felt she wanted to say something. I waited.

'There's a reason I have Wednesdays off.' I saw her take a deep breath. 'Every Wednesday, I see a man. A man I love. It is our day.'

'He loves you?'

'Oh yes. We've been together for almost twenty-five years.'

'Just Wednesday?'

'He's married with children.'

Her life had been structured for this man. Her life was dedicated to him. He had a family and children, and her every Wednesday. She had never seen anyone else. He was her love. No holidays with him, weekends, birthdays, Christmas, just Wednesdays. I listened, asking the occasional question. Over the next weeks I heard more. She met him at the same small hotel at 8.00 am and he left in the evening. They hung out, as my son would say now. She knew very little about his life.

She had no telephone number for him or for where he worked. He rarely bought her presents, and never gave her money, but she could stay the Wednesday night in the hotel if she chose.

An unpaid courtesan. She did not accumulate wealth, he was the prize. She loved him and he was enough, and it was all on his terms.

One Thursday she came to work and was visibly upset. When she became upset she was rude to customers. We were busy so I picked up her slack in the store. She didn't come back after lunch. I covered for her.

On Friday she told me he hadn't turned up at the hotel.

She got more distressed day by day as there was no word from him and she couldn't contact him.

I started to field complaints about her rudeness. I didn't know what to do. I held her secret.

After three weeks she solved the mystery of his absence. I never found out how she did.

She came in to work and told me. He had died of a heart attack. The funeral had come and gone and she had not known.

Her rage and grief were palpable, and I didn't know how to help her. I was powerless.

Then one day HR came into the department and she went off for a meeting with them. She returned for her belongings.

'I've been fired.' She walked away inconsolable, in a wave of rage and grief.

I was alone in the department standing useless beside the till. She went and I didn't follow her.

I never saw her again.

She had been a compliant handmaiden. A devotee with no rights.

She made the choice and sacrifice, but she had not been trained or empowered to show her rage to him, her demands were silent. He must have believed he was enough, that a Wednesday was enough and that she should be grateful for it.

Did he know or care about her loneliness and the sacrifices? That she had no choice and only rage at his death?

'You can't have your cake and eat it.'

In *The Trojan Women* by Euripides, after the destruction of Troy, the privileged women wait to hear their fate. Polyxena – the youngest daughter of Hecuba and Priam – understands this sacrifice. She has served as a priestess, a handmaiden to Zeus, and he has betrayed them all. They have built temples, burned incense, devoted their lives to him, and he has abandoned their sacred bond.

Handmaidens serve someone they feel is superior to them. A God, or for some women, a love. Handmaidens are not equal, and we have lived as handmaidens for centuries in the hope that we won't be betrayed. This subject is so important that I have written a chapter, Chapter 17, about it.

I met *The Eumenides* in some of the women I taught in Holloway Women's Prison. The women had murdered their male abusers. When they started to stab these men they couldn't stop. Male law was horrified that these women stabbed not once but many, many times. All the stored abuse forcing their arm and the knife in their hand to plunge down again and again. The savagery of the attack mostly impacted their sentencing. It was harsher because men couldn't understand it. We store our rage because we know it makes us both ugly and vulnerable to men.

It is simple. The rage was tamed for so long that when released it was unquenchable. The Furies, tireless in pursuit of justice for women. Of course they couldn't stop. No man can stop when they start punching their bully. That image is one of Hollywood's great male underdog stories, glorious and worshipped by all. But not for women.

If women don't show their rage it will somehow come out after years of blockage and is then unstoppable, or it is turned against a woman's own body. I witnessed this in my early teaching in Holloway but the opposite at the male prison, Pentonville. When male prisoners get upset they release outwardly. Hitting, fighting and smashing their cells.

In Holloway I began to notice how the rage these women felt was pulled towards themselves. They cut themselves and openly spoke to me about how it eased their fury.

It clarified what I had witnessed, particularly in Nanna.

In the library where I worked in 1972 after the department store, I began to recognize how women's spiritual voices had been silenced. This was through a life-changing meeting and friendship with a Reverend – the Rev as he was called.

The Rev was well into his eighties. Scruffy, often unshaven, not hygienic. A hardly white dog collar loose around his scraggy neck. A few teeth left. Bright eyes. I loved being on the desk when he came in.

The books he was reading were so intriguing. We started to talk. He knew things I wanted to know.

His story was that he had been a Roman Catholic priest, but his views and studies had been intolerable to them. Now the Anglican Church had given him a home. He conducted services when deputies were required. I heard him preach – it was good, and it was dangerous and exciting. He was a brilliant, anarchic scholar and theologian. He read Greek, Aramaic, Hebrew and Nabataean Aramaic.

He translated some of the Dead Sea Scrolls and introduced me to the Gnostic Gospels.

He was the first person I ever heard say that the Church should have been given to Mary Magdalene. The first man I'd met to be outraged by the way the Christian Church had treated women. We started to have lunch and tea dates. There was nothing sexual or creepy, he just wanted to help answer my questions.

The other staff couldn't understand.

'He smells.'

'He's interesting.'

He was patient and passionate. He shared words and how they had been translated, and the subtle changes of meaning, which pushed the Christian belief into a place that squashed women's equality.

'There are two words for Virgin,' he explained to me. 'One means sexually pure. The other means spiritually pure.'

Mary was spiritually pure.

'Jesus doesn't say, "I am the way, the truth, the life." He says, "I am a way, a truth, a life."'

Of course: editing.

This was 1972. This wasn't conventional or trendy thought at that time, but an old man outraged by the treatment of both Marys.

Once he wrote a name on a scrap of paper for me – *Karl Jaspers*. A psychiatrist and philosopher. I stuffed the paper into my pocket. After that meeting, the Rev was absent for some weeks, and I eventually heard that he had died and that his papers had been taken into the care of the Anglican Church.

I realize now that I had met an enlightened man. A man who swam against the tide of political, social, cultural and spiritual beliefs. A man who knew the truth about the real equality of women and the abuse done to them. One of the Rev's key rages was that women were kept out of the highest levels of spiritual practice – the speaking of sacred texts and the ability to lead worship and rituals. This was long before the ordination of women in the Anglican Church. This thrilled me.

His belief was that the speaking of sacred words changes you, that the physical quality of words when spoken aloud could heal you, and that women should be allowed that transformation and healing.

After his death I started to read Karl Jaspers. The search that Jaspers's work triggered in me was around what he called, 'The Axial Age.' This was an Age (500–300 BCE) that produced or birthed all the current, powerful, world religions and philosophies (Hinduism, Buddhism, the Hebrew Prophets, Confucianism and the Greek philosophers). All barring women from the sacred.

Was this the key? The moment women's spiritual voices were banned they lost their power in society.

The Rev reminded me of questions I had asked when I was younger. The question I asked a teacher after morning prayers and the singing of my favourite hymn, *Dear Lord and Father of Mankind.* I had looked around the hall and there were no men so: 'Why don't we sing "Dear Lady Mother of Womankind?"'

I was eleven and the question didn't go down well. This was sealed further in my mind in 1976, when Merlin Stone's book, *When God Was a Woman*, came out. I remember reading this on the upper deck of a bus slowly progressing up Upper Street in Islington. I looked up and out of the window, as many of my life's experiences came into focus differently.

Much later, my friend, the actress Olympia Dukakis, got hold of me. It was 1999. I received a startling text from her. She had an Ancient Fragment of a Persian play. Very early – 5,000 years ago. She wanted to work on it with me. There was one short scene that she had had translated. The play is set in a time when women had full spiritual power, perhaps all power. The priestesses are in the Temple in the Holy of Holies. The women are the ordained doorways to the Divine. In the play, the men violently break down the doors to the women's inner sanctuary and begin to do what some men do: rape, disfigure and violently attack the priestesses. One man removes the sacrificial knife from the high alter, holds the High Priestess on the ground, takes the knife and forces her to hold it. He then bends her arm and hand so that the knife points into her womb and says to her 'Turn your power on yourself.'

That's all; the fragment of an ancient play.

I had a flashback to a beautiful, young girl I had helped with learning to read in Holloway who, in her rage and despair, cut one of her own nipples off.

In the event, Olympia and I never worked on this, we never found the time. Later, I talked to an eminent scholar about the fragment.

'Don't touch it,' he said. 'It will curse you!'

Before I began my training at The Royal Central School I had known my journey in life was about words, poetry, Shakespeare, theatre and the political repression of women.

I didn't know it was about voice until the first few weeks of training.

I spoke poetry in public and was rather pleased that within the first weeks we were asked to bring a poem of our own choice into class.

I chose *Dulce et Decorum Est* by Wilfred Owen, the brilliant First World War poet who died a few days before peace was declared.

The teacher I am describing is not the great Gerard Benson, who also taught me poetry, but a man who was not a regular.

As I spoke Owen's words, I saw that slight, male smirk all women have experienced. I thought I spoke it well. He didn't talk about my work. He – still with the smirk coating the tone of his voice – suggested that only a man could speak Owen.

'Why?' I knew he was beginning to dislike me intensely.

'Because women don't fight in war so you can't imagine what it's like.'

'Have you fought in a war?'

He was already signalling for the next student to get up.

I got louder. 'Have you fought in a war?'

'No.'

'So you can't speak this poem, can you?'

Sigh. Still the smirk.

'Are you saying women can only speak poems written by women and men can only speak poems written by men?'

The smirk was fading.

'No.'

'So, what are you saying?'

'I think that you could speak Owen but from the point of view of the girl waiting for her young man in England.'

I felt that terrifying energy gather in my stomach. The fury building. The Furies entering my body.

'That's ridiculous! That's not respecting the poem. The words, the situation. It's about being there, in the mud, seeing death – not sitting by a fire with a cup of tea waiting for your fiancé to return!'

The energy was out of the bag and I couldn't put it back now.

I saw him prepare to hurt me. Really hurt me. He had taken the blow I had delivered and had recovered enough to retaliate. The smirk was back, bigger, more pronounced.

'What you haven't yet understood is that a woman's physical voice can never compete with a man's. Your voice cannot express the full horror of war.'

I was down on the canvas.

The next student got up.

It was a crossroads. He had inadvertently given me my path.

Words, feelings, ideas and spirit, yes. But it all manifests through the voice.

This was going to be my study, not just for women but for anyone who didn't feel the right to speak or to be present. Anyone who had an important story to tell.

The voice.

One dreadful teacher, teaching with the joy of destroying rather than re-empowering a student, handed me my path and my pilgrimage.

11
VOCATION

The life so short, the craft so long to learn.

Chaucer

I knew that it would be a long, hard journey, and that I would have to be diligent and single-minded.

In the days after my brush with the smirking, poetry teacher, I knew I would have to learn how to teach well – not just voice, but the craft of teaching.

I knew I had to work on my own voice.

I knew I had to find out about as many aspects of voice as I could. I knew that I had to work with anyone – not just singers and actors. I knew that I had to understand the history of women's education and how they had been taught to express themselves.

But first I had to find out why a woman's voice became so reduced when it started out so released. Why women displayed weaker voices and less powerful presences. Why the full-throated singing of Nanna in her last days of life wasn't how she vocally lived.

And my mother's full vocal power of despair and grief as she was leaving.

I remembered how she had given birth to my brother at home. I remembered the night before his birth, her scrubbing the kitchen floor on her knees to prepare the nest. My sister and I were woken in the morning by Father with the announcement of John's arrival. We ran to see him and Mother, all cleaned up in the marriage bed.

It was years later she and I had the conversation.

'Isn't it strange we didn't hear you giving birth to John?'

And in her simple, unsentimental way she said, 'I didn't make a sound as I didn't want to frighten you.'

'You held all that pain in?'

A nod.

My mother had been 'taught' well. Not to disturb.

It was early in my teaching that I would differentiate between the natural voice and the habitual voice.

Student – standing slumped, shallow breath: 'This is how I naturally stand.'

Student – hardly audible: 'This is my natural voice.'

To which I learned to reply: 'No, it's your *habitual* voice. These are habits blocking your full natural and powerful voice.'

Then I began to notice that for many women, their full natural, powerful voice and presence scared them, and made them feel revealed, exposed and noticed. Their habits had become masks, placed over their natural selves, and were mostly protections. Their power had been unrewarded, or worse, punished.

So, some men and all women I have ever taught need a safe place to find their natural voice.

And it has to be an active choice.

Their mask has been, and often still is, a tool of survival, and cannot be removed without a clear decision from them. And alongside that decision they must be encouraged, and not reprimanded if they have to return to the habit.

Losing your natural presence and voice.

To be, or not to be, that is the question.

Hamlet

The reason this line resonates with all of us, is that Shakespeare is talking about being present and choosing to be.

Physical, emotional, intellectual and spiritual impacts destroy our natural presence and voice. Events knock us out of balance and wounds enter our bodies and embed. Impacts can land so powerfully that we can lose ourselves and therefore our presence.

Sticks and stones may break my bones, but words will never hurt me. This isn't true. Particularly if they come on a very regular basis. When this happens, we close down and absent ourselves by moving into the First Circle or hitting out at the world in the Third Circle.

The slings and arrows of outrageous fortune. These you either suffer or choose to oppose.

Life will deal blows, *the whips and scorns of time, the oppressor's wrong, the proud man's contumely, the pangs of disprized love, the law's delay, the insolence of office.* It is Hamlet that lists these impacts that reduce us. But he was a man, and a powerful and highly privileged one.

No one gets through life without a blow or two. Privileged men arguably receive fewer than less privileged men.

Women of all stations feel these impacts harder.

There are an abundance of stories that analyse a man's resistance and resilience in overcoming 'outrageous fortune', but there are too few about women – maybe the world doesn't expect women to recover from such impacts.

For thousands of years women have had to develop survival techniques that mask their natural presence and voice. Anyone who is not in power has to do this, or choose to be an outsider.

For women, our beauty, our intelligence, our creativity and our articulacy still threaten, and our choice to mask or not to mask is a moment to moment one. To reveal is to risk punishment.

Survival often employs masks.

Smiling when you don't want to smile.

Agreeing when you don't want to agree.

Flattering. Flirting, pretending you are less intelligent than you are.

Working on pleasing and trying to be liked by people you dislike.

All these strategies are absolutely understandable after thousands of years of oppression and potential punishment.

Only Connect!

E.M. Forster

Everything you are is connected to everything in the world and in yourself.

Your full presence in the world, which is connected to you being present in yourself, is dependent on the full, natural freedom and strength of your body, breath and voice systems connecting to each other.

You are in your full power and presence when you are connected to the whole of yourself. Body, mind, heart and spirit connected, not divided and fragmented.

Every unnecessary physical tension in your body – however small – impacts your presence in yourself and in the world. What you give and what you receive is reduced. Every unnecessary tension dampens our ability to listen and respond to what we hear.

Every unnecessary physical tension impedes your breath, which impedes your voice range, resonance and speech, and impedes your ability to think and to feel and make any engagement with the world around you.

An interesting exercise is to look at photos of yourself from a child into early adulthood. You might begin to see the tell-tale signs of how you were diminished and when you began to lose your power.

I look at myself as a four-year-old girl, posing by a table my brother still has. A photographer had been hired to take portraits of my sister and myself. A nearly natural smile. A reserve. Early signs of my, still, shyness. I am present but wary. There is a slight retreat in my body. Maybe I didn't like the forced pleasantness of the photographer. Maybe I could feel his wariness of me not responding. I would always feel the preference men had for my sister, who was more outgoing.

The reserve continues as I examine myself getting older.

Always present, but not enough to be perceived as a provocateur – which I certainly was in my mind.

My early memories of my father are of knowing that he wasn't present at home. The leader's presence is contagious, so the house changed its energy when he returned from work. He was present if he could be funny, which normally meant you had to be amused by his jokes. I wasn't. The jokes were repetitive and laughter was always expected.

He loved my mother, so she sometimes had his full presence; my sister could flirt and please him, so she was safe. No presence for Nanna as she wasn't amused, and, although frightened of him, had the courage not to give way to her fear and dependency on him. I had unconditional love and presence from my mother and Nanna, so my sense of self stayed intact, and by the age of nine I had learnt to become a very present nuisance to my father.

As I grew older, my body and presence were not diminished.

Partly because I was very good at sports that encouraged physical ease, rhythm and breath: tennis and lacrosse. Both of these sports keep a centred body.

The other reason I stayed centred in my body was that the time I grew up in, the 1950s, didn't worship perfection or sexualize children. All the girls at school wore sensible shoes and clothes, and only a few tried to wear make-up. The body was not so eulogized or so abused with food, cigarettes, drugs and booze. It was much easier to keep centred in the 1950s and early 1960s.

What I can see in the photo is the presence of a resting tiger.

A presence hungry for knowledge and much too serious to be liked by many. Both staff and peers found my gravitas tedious, and somehow I didn't care.

I didn't need to be liked and that isn't popular with boys – or girls. I had a keen interest in books and would now be called a nerd, and I was often demeaned by teachers as being over ambitious for a girl!

This did affect how and when I used my voice. I mumbled when I had to chit-chat. The informal was muttered and then, I was 'too passionate' when I was engaged in serious conversation. My passion sounded rude to many, but the few staff who understood passion cared deeply for me. My voice could always work when it mattered.

There was some solace in the drama class. We only did classics so that was fine for me. Shakespeare and poetry.

In the photos of my childhood I can see the strength and stubbornness, and an overwhelming desire to survive, which has been and probably still is mistaken for arrogance.

I can see I need love, and therefore the fluidity of vulnerability.

Now I can see that later, openness would be unlocked in me through loss and grief. The battering on my heart that allowed empathy and compassion to enter the young girl fighting for an equal voice.

It was partly encounters in being taught and teaching that opened me up. There are many doors into the same room. Find many doors in your work to show the door to the student and they will show a door they have found and teach you back.

I started teaching at exactly the moment in history when women gained legal equality in the UK. That gave my work a political urgency, and I couldn't understand why women's voices and power did not move faster. Nor could I understand, later, why the female students who had been born after 1975 felt no urgency to speak powerfully: it was as if their equality was a given and didn't require work.

This was in direct opposition to pre-equality women, who knew they had to be clear and articulate to be taken seriously.

Throughout the late eighties and then the nineties, young women would tell me that they didn't have to work on this, because *we are equal now*. It wasn't until the 2000s that younger women realized that they, too, had to work on the way they communicated if they wanted to be heard.

Part of the backlash of anger from men is that they don't have to pretend any more that they're interested in us.

The most articulate women come from worlds where men have not agreed to, or don't pretend to agree with, their equality. The stakes are higher and the contempt from men unmasked, as it had been for me in my youth.

At the moment I write this, in 2022, I am more optimistic than I have ever been about the young women I work with. They are prepared to work and excel with their voice and their language, and do not expect sympathy, or play the damsel in distress.

When I began to teach, all voice work with women – unless you were an actress or singer – was elocution. There was nothing to do with the body or breath or tapping into the magnificence of the full and free voice.

For men it was more physical, and their natural voice wasn't as squashed. Men were *expected* to use their voice.

The simplest strategy in keeping power, is to deny those who threaten your education. Any study of the complete documentation of all debates in Parliament at the time of the Education Acts of the mid-nineteenth century, reveal the fear that the privileged few feel about educating the masses: and at the time of these debates only working-class men were being considered. Women are not mentioned.

The problem for the privileged was that the industrialization of Britain meant that working-class men had to be educated. Efficiency required that some of them had to be taught reading, writing and simple arithmetic. This would enable mass production.

There are clear records of considerable worry among the Victorian Tories that reading and writing were dangerous to teach to the working classes; but, in the end, the economic advantages were considered worth the risk.

The size of the state school classes – 150 – meant learning was done by rote. The humanities, the use of voice and the formality of debate and structured argument, was impossible to teach in such huge classes. What the upper-class Victorians knew from their own education and through a direct link from ancient received wisdom, was that voice – and formal structure of presentation – was, and is, power in leadership.

Voice and rhetoric is essential to anyone interested in power.

Of course, less privileged but brilliant, young boys were spotted by astute teachers, and ways were found to send them to Oxbridge. Thomas Hardy's *Jude the Obscure* is a heart-wrenching account of this scenario. The sacrifice was, and sometimes still is, huge.

Young girls were also educated and, like my nanna, some with very fine and diligent minds were chosen to be teachers, not to go to university.

There have always been brilliant, resilient and courageous young, working-class men who have wriggled through all the blockages of their background to flourish and find their proper place at the table of power. More astounding though are the women who, against greater odds and greater losses, have done the same; and that has had to include finding their voice and honouring the power of formal speech.

It was in the late 1970s that I started to realize that the education of women's voices was hard, and much of what I found then still exists for many women during their education.

The first time I was asked to teach only voice to a group of women who weren't actors was at a finishing school in London. Girls from wealthy families, dressed in designer fashion and being 'finished'.

My brief was simple: they should be audible and clear so that they could get a wealthy husband. They should entertain their husbands and not challenge them.

The headmistress of the school made it clear to me that the men they would marry did not need them to be serious or have opinions. She expressed this most firmly.

'The men they meet don't want to hear their ideas. These men like to be the ones with all the opinions. The girls must entertain, listen attentively and agree with the men.'

I was told they would be marrying captains of industry, and I was expected to teach them to support the men's views and to keep pleasant conversations going, to cover up any rudeness that their husbands might display. Chit-chat would bore their husbands, so it was incumbent on their wives to deal with any 'boring' guests.

This was in 1976.

Many leaders – and some are now women – hate the informality of chit-chat, and entering a space where this form of communication is necessary. And many are deeply relieved if they have partners who can keep light, unprovocative conversations going.

The headmistress said that the girls should be able to open a *fête*, introduce a speaker and be an exemplary hostess, clearly introducing guests that would appreciate each other, and know when the gentlemen would like the women to leave so that business could be discussed.

I had experienced this in the sixties and seventies at dinner parties with my father, obeying the ritualized moment when the hostess gracefully gets up from the table to shepherd the women into the drawing room to drink coffee and leave the men with their port and important discussions. But I had thought that was a dying era.

When I suggested some content work and rhetoric to focus their voices, she firmly said, 'No, no. Too hard for them and not useful.'

I was shown around this beautiful building in Kensington.

In one large, magnificent room I was invited to watch the class. Fourteen well-dressed young women, aged between eighteen and twenty, were being put through some essential physical paces.

In the centre of the room was a stage that had steps on each side. On the stage was a lectern and one high-backed, elegant chair. At the side of the room was part of a car. On closer examination, I realized that this was the back seat of a Bentley. The back door could be opened and the seat was well upholstered. The class consisted of the girls queuing up to practise walking elegantly up the steps on one side of the stage; stopping at the lectern to look out and smile at the audience; then practising sitting on the chair with ease and good posture and keeping the knees, thighs and calf muscles clamped together. Then to stand up and progress across the stage and down the other steps. Then they would move to the slice of car. The teacher would open the back door and they would practise getting into the car elegantly, not showing their knickers. The door was shut and then opened so that they could get out of the car without any undesired revelation of underwear.

The loop of girls would go round and round like this for the whole class, all the time with the vivacious, male teacher correcting any lack of elegance.

Actors will often practise in a similar way if a stage entrance or prop is difficult to handle. But these girls were practising in order to get a husband.

I expected to find the girls I met annoying, but instead, I found beautifully dressed, vulnerable and passively furious young women.

The first impression was that they all carried that peculiar boredom and weariness of the entitled, particularly the entitled who have no passion on their horizons. No love on the go, no intellectual pursuit, no cause to care about; no reason really to get up in the morning except to put on the latest fashions. They didn't have the distractions of technology so they were bereft.

They had all been told they were dim.

I imagined that they had, in their earlier schooling, been in classes with bright and driven peers and hadn't kept up. Their parents, having no pride or care in their exam results, were spending money to give them some cosmetic appeal and manners.

A few, at the back of the class, obviously were bright, but sat sulking. Rebels, hating all their education and maybe all the missed opportunities of intellectual engagement. But many of them seemed pleased with themselves for being stupid. The tone when some women say they are stupid can sound as though they are proud of ignorance: 'I'm so stupid!' said with self-mockery and an expectance of applause.

I know that this is a defence strategy, and one that makes some men find these girls appealing.

But this was the first time I had heard women admitting so readily to 'stupidity'. That would not have been tolerated at my school.

This glimpse of pride in ignorance and stupidity gathered momentum in the eighties and nineties, and many female students of mine made similar announcements, sometimes in a direct challenge to feminism, but also as a kind of laziness, and a rejection of taking responsibility for the fineness of their minds.

The first time a student tells me that they are stupid, I say 'I don't believe you are.' I made a similar statement to these young women and immediately got some spark of attention from them. It was as if no one had ever said that to them; and they relaxed and began to work.

I followed the brief and taught them to use their voice and be clear. I gave them structured writing and powerful poems that I encouraged them to discuss. They enjoyed the challenge and I noticed that some were buying poetry anthologies. They were creatively struggling with the language, structures and ideas. I noticed too that as the discussions got deeper and they began to express powerful ideas, they would immediately mock or laugh at themselves, or giggle or wiggle their way out of a profound insight. They punished themselves before they could be punished.

They also found it hard to be succinct and clear without a long preamble. Were they just getting into the idea, finding it out for themselves? Having to speak at length before they knew what they knew? Or were they justifying the idea before saying it?

With one group, who got very engaged, we debated this.

They thought both strategies made them 'ramble on'. One used those words as a quote from her father about her mother: 'Your mother rambles on.'

We all ramble when we express a new idea and search for words. And also when we feel we aren't being listened to or heard. The more practise you get at expressing yourself aloud, the less you ramble. Girls ramble because they don't get the time or space to practise aloud. Many teachers still give boys more time than girls to take centre stage with an important idea. If you allow a speaker to repeat the idea again immediately, they self-edit and become noticeably more structured and succinct.

I quoted William Hazlitt (1778–1830), '*His sayings are generally like women's letters: all the pith is in the postscript.*'

That got them going.

One day I asked the question I had been thinking all along.

'Why do you always seem bored?'

Silence . . . followed by laughter. Then one of the very bright, initially sulky ones, said: 'It's safe to be bored.'

'But if you seem bored you will attract people who like you to be boring.' I could see that I had her attention. 'You get what you give in life. Please show interest, show interest in life.'

I was called to the headmistress's office to discuss my progress.

Bugger. This was the highest hourly rate I had ever been paid.

She eyed me askance.

'The girls are enjoying your classes. What are you working on?'

'I am working on them not rambling or being tedious in their explanations.' Near enough to the truth, I thought.

'What do you mean by rambling?'

'They know what they want to say but take so much time to get there.'

'No! You mustn't do that. Their husbands will enjoy them not knowing too quickly what they think, and they will enjoy teaching those skills to their wives. Men like to steer young women, not to be challenged. You don't understand, Patsy: these young women need powerful men. They can't survive without them. Their parents know this, which is why they are here. These girls are not capable of being independent.'

I taught a year in Kensington. I wasn't asked back for a second year!

The headmistress was the first female teacher I had met that was a handmaiden to male power. A female enabler of women's disempowerment.

There were no such teachers at my school or at The Royal Central School, and for that I am most grateful.

Things have changed since the late seventies – but not as much as you would think.

I teach in schools all over the UK, and in mixed-sex schools all the traits from the finishing school are still present.

The teachers encourage all the pupils to speak out, but the girls that do are often playing for laughs, or mocking themselves after expressing a strong and good idea. They take longer to get to the point, to give back detail to furnish a point with more examples before stating the point. They often ramble, and you can feel the group getting bored; but there is a control in speaking too long and boring a group. It is not powerful, but at least it gets you noticed.

The girls who get into communication first are generally louder and less serious than the girls who are interested in deep knowledge: those girls stay silent. They get on with their work. Keep their heads below the parapets, developing thoughts and knowledge but not practising using their voice.

These are the silent and brilliant girls who should get into Oxbridge but who haven't yet practised their physical voice for the rigorous interviews.

I coach some of the most impressive women leaders to trust what they know, and say what they know, without preamble or multiple examples of how they know what they know, and I teach them not to justify what they know. To be direct and to the point, to not waste time.

I then coach them to stop laughing at themselves for being brilliant and talented – because that allows the men to laugh at them too. I teach them not to mock themselves. To speak to the point sooner rather than later, and not to be ashamed of their knowledge. Not to allow men to steer them at a meeting or ignore them. And to never let anybody take and state their hard-earned knowledge as if it's their own.

12
VOICE AND RHETORIC

Western culture is directly connected to Ancient Greek civilization.

When I was fifteen, thanks to Mrs Breakey, I experienced the visceral shock of discovering that Plato didn't discuss women's ability to love in *The Symposium*. To admit women loved fully, I realized, would be to admit to their equal humanity. I remember thinking that this omission was rather like being taught in the 1950s that animals didn't feel. The concept is that even the cow bellowing as her calf is taken to be slaughtered is not feeling maternal despair.

I was six, standing with my mother in the Northumberland countryside. She had taken me to see the pit ponies. These ponies had been retired from working underground in the coal mines and were spending their few remaining years pain free, in a field. My mother was openly moved by their last years of freedom, and as we stood watching them, we were joined by a stranger, an ex-miner, who agreed with her. This man explained how it always broke his heart to see how they were treated, and he was always glad that they were granted a few years in a field above ground at the end of their lives.

'They love as well as we do,' he said. 'Most believe they don't, but they love.'

Silence. My mother's breath relaxed.

'I know,' she replied.

'I suppose you couldn't put them underground like that if you thought they loved,' he said.

I was not included in this conversation. I had not begun to read about how races have been demonized in order to justify genocide, but in my young brain this idea, although initially scrambled, became an important thought to ponder. If you believe that a species, a gender or a person could not love as well or as equally as you, that gives you permission to punish them.

Plato has given the world tremendous wisdom, but he didn't believe that women could love equally, and Western society has that premise buried in its deepest structures: the idea that the fineness and clarity of a man's ability to love is superior to a woman's.

In Ancient Greek theatres, the actors were men, and the stories highlighted the danger of women's power and showed the destruction of powerful women.

The theatre, then, was a more sophisticated lad's dressing room. The men nodding at the transgressions of male dominance and women's part in the men's destruction. The stories supported their democracy's drive to cage women and drain them of all their power.

The state controlled writers and thinkers. The great philosopher, Socrates, was ordered to drink hemlock when his ideas were deemed to be corrupting youth. The great playwrights, Aeschylus, Sophocles and Euripides, would have known that any clear expression of not supporting their state paymasters would be severely punished.

No one knows exactly what these writers actually thought about women, but there are clues. Some might have had compassion and a sense of unease when thy wrote about female destruction. Greek civilization was clear in its fear of women's power and its disgust for it. It wasn't wrapped in any form of disguise. The Amazons were fabled, female warriors and all Greek men knew they had to be subdued or destroyed. It was pure terror and hatred of women.

Kept indoors, sent off to weave and spin, expected to wait patiently for years for the return of their husbands, put on pedestals when beautiful and then hated for their power over men's desire. Helen of Troy was blamed for the carnage done by men and faced being stoned to death.

Andromache had been an exemplary wife to Hector, which is why all the Greeks wanted her. You are damned if you have your sexual power and damned if you behave well and honourably.

Women must not win.

They must be tamed by force, rape, disfigurement or the deprivation of their freedom. Lock them up; if they are beautiful, worship them, or if the beautiful girls don't find you attractive, rape them.

And don't educate them.

Before the Greek democracy there was an aristocracy that was kinder to privileged women, and it also produced the writer that all male, Greek poets thought was the greatest of them all – Sappho: a woman.

Only snatches of her work remain, but we know of her excellence because later male writers eulogize her.

So the Greeks did know that women could write.

They particularly remark on her forms. And form is part of rhetoric, and rhetoric gives the physical voice and words power, potency and excitement.

Rhetoric is the art of effective and persuasive speaking. The word literally means *to move*. To move others when you communicate, to move yourself, to move the body, mind, heart and spirit. To move ideas along. To ask questions and to seek answers.

Rhetoric is a description of codes and patterns that we can use to focus and transform others as we speak. Forms, rhythms, pace and qualities of language that help speakers to move and change an audience.

Rhetoric has always been taught to privileged men. But if you haven't had this education, the word can frighten and alienate many.

I understand that it has a rigid if not frigid resonance in many minds, but I feel strongly that rhetoric attempts to codify the physical forms of sound, rhythm and structure that is in the human DNA.

Rhetoric is *of us* and facilitates powerful storytelling. Every great speech that has moved an audience or changed the world can be analysed to find all the rhetorical forms that the speaker has often quite organically instinctively used.

It is not to be so adhered to that it becomes stuffy, but it is a door through which one can step, to teach and learn the spoken word, to be as effective and as physical as possible. Rules to be learned and, sometimes, broken.

This human code of effective storytelling was developed in Athens, but we now know that because the Greeks were trading with so many other civilizations, they inevitably took on, and built on, stories and rhetorical forms from them.

The Ancient Greeks knew that democracy could only exist if every free Athenian man was ready and able to stand in the Assembly and argue effectively for or against legislation.

A man's power was reliant on his ability to speak to, and transform, an audience, and therefore was a critical part of education.

In the fifth century BC, schools that taught rhetoric opened in Athens. These schools were for privileged men only. When the Romans conquered Greece, they began to develop and build on the codes of effective speaking.

Rhetoric is based on three connected stages of work.

1. Delivery

The ability to be present and use your body, breath, voice and speech to effectively deliver an important idea, story or debate. The student was taught that to have authority they had to stand fully centred, maintain clear eye contact, breathe deeply and low to power words into space, and support a free and full voice with range and resonance. Delivery is the craft I initially teach, and it produces an audible, clear and expressive voice that can thrill and inspire an audience. Speech muscles, strong and flexible to deliver clarity, change of pace and rhythm within and through the words.

Not much was written about delivery. Partly because the privileged, male students had not lost their natural presence and voice, and their lifestyle had not eroded their connection to language. Also, because they knew they would often be speaking to unsympathetic listeners, students were taught that they must delight the ear of the audience with their delivery. Before you can deliver any idea or feeling, you need your presence, body and voice. These young men continually used their voices, so they never lost them. They just had to be enhanced. The training of delivery was to sound authentic, not embellished or poetic.

After delivery comes form.

2. Rhetorical form

Form is not cosmetic but is embedded in us.

When your vocal instrument is free enough to deliver, you can then concentrate on entertaining an audience with reason and feeling, and compel them to listen, change and even agree with you. Rhetorical form and storytelling is in our DNA. Simply, if you read or tell a child a good story, and they can hear you clearly, they organically feel what works in terms of form. They are learning rhetoric as you read to them.

If you speak well-structured text aloud, you understand rhetoric.

There has been such mystery around rhetoric.

Of course, there have always been extremely talented storytellers who weren't from the privileged classes, or men who understood the need to deliver, delight, entertain and change an audience and who used rhetoric without knowing the word.

My nanna had not been taught rhetoric, but like many uneducated women, figured it out and had the courage, in front of me, to display her skills. The renowned actor Robert Edison, famed for his verse speaking, said to me, 'If one listens to the audience, one will know if one is audible or interesting. You know about form because you can feel it work – the effect of form is felt in the audience.'

I think of Nanna and her sharp comment that hit a truth in me. That Shakespeare wrote what 'we said': for Nanna 'we' meant the working classes. She understood that form and rhetoric are not academic pursuits, but ones all storytellers know.

There is considerable evidence that the educated have always taken ideas from folklore: the traditions of the working classes. Folk dances were tidied and cleaned up and evolved into courtly dances. The source dance was beautified and then owned by the upper classes. Folk music and ballads suffered the same fate. The privileged were also tamed as they stole folk dances and stories. What had been joyously free dance and speaking became held, poised and 'elegant'. Troubadours, clowns and fools brought dangerous and bawdy stories to the court, and these stories were snapped up and 'civilized'. The middle classes read fairy stories in the nineteenth century that had been diluted from ancient versions, making the stories less sexual and violent.

All these folk creations were structured: they had rhythm, pace and repetition, and a beginning and an ending. The stories had form and pathos, ethos and logos: feelings, ethics and logic. I will write about how you can fully understand these terms and embody this work later in the book.

If, as we know, the privileged stole stories and dances from the working classes and made them tamer, we can strongly speculate that the stories of women were treated in the same way by the men who heard them.

The actor Emma Thompson once speculated that all the 'anonymous' poems were written by women.

Form, in communication, contains and moves the ideas and feelings forward.

Form contains and clarifies the emotional cost of the story.

The simplest example is *Once upon a time . . . And they all lived happily ever after*. This naïve form enables us to bear the horror or grief within the story with the knowledge that it will end happily. Form contains and makes unbearable stories just bearable.

But form does something else equally necessary when we tell difficult and important stories. It moves the action forward. It encourages the storyteller not to dwell emotionally, but to move forward through it and seek resolution to continue surviving and living. In this way rhythm is form and the rhythm has, within it, pace. A structured piece of writing is like a musical score that moves the speaker forward at different speeds.

The most basic rhythm is iambic – Greek for foot, a dance step. *de-Dum* – unstressed into stressed.

To be or not to be – de-Dum, de-Dum, de-Dum.

This rhythm is of us – it is the heartbeat. *de-Dum*. The first rhythm and last rhythm all men and women hear. The heartbeat or iambic is not only a rhythm that the educated understand. This rhythm is the life force, and takes us forward when we speak. Up and out: *de-Dum*. Blood pumping and circulating.

The iambic is expressed in the syllables of speech. It is the basic rhythm in form. But because life shocks us and our heart, the rhythm in spoken text changes to match the change in us. It is not always regular. The heart shudders, misses a beat, recovers stasis by shifting from the regular iambic heartbeat to other rhythms.

The iambic reveals stress, pace and the moments when the rhythm and pace are broken: it speeds up, or it slows down, or it breaks.

3. Sequential thought and language

Anthropologists say one of the great moments that allowed Homo Sapiens to take over the planet was the growth in our brains so we could think sequentially: 'Look, deer prints in the earth: they are going that way, towards the lake. Let's follow the deer.'

Six stages of thought moving forward.

This hunting sequence is exactly the same thinking journey as:

To be or not to be: That is the question.

Three stages of thinking, moving forward.

This sequential thought journey was termed 'classical thinking', and, like opening up a Russian doll, the sequence is seeking an outcome, a resolve – an understanding. A child opening the doll is engaging in the physical process of an action to find the centre of an object.

We are doing the same thing when we use words and ideas to resolve an issue or solve a problem. And the finding of words and ideas is made concrete as we speak them aloud: the physicality of speaking clarifies the brain.

The term *Classical* has encouraged many people to feel that it is an elite skill, not an inherent human one. Anyone can practise and hone it to be a powerful weapon in debate, storytelling and building a dialogue, or in discussions that seek resolution and conclusion. We can all make a journey towards the deer!

If you read classical texts aloud, you can feel and uncover this sequence. And as you speak these texts, you can exercise the brain to strengthen and enhance your ability to think and express yourself in formed thoughts moving forward. Until recently, very few women were taught or encouraged to think and speak in this way. Some women chose to enter a convent in order to be allowed to think and study the classics, and explore the breadth and depth of thoughts and feelings.

Other common forms of the many rhetorical possibilities that we all use include:

Repetition – All stories and powerful ideas use repetition to highlight potent messages in the story and build expectancy in the audience. *'I have a dream . . .'*

Antithesis – The conflict of opposites. The two sides of an argument. The conflict in the heart and the mind seeking understanding. *Such civil war is in my love and hate*. Love versus hate. *And see the brave day sunk in hideous night*. Day versus night, with 'brave' versus 'hideous'.

Children use this in stories and in exploring the fairness of the world: *this* versus *that*. This swing in thought and heart develops and complicates, and then helps us understand what we think and feel.

Content – Rhetoric also has terms to describe the nature and quality of the story that form contains.

When you tell or find stories that respect, challenge, educate or change others you are using one or all of these three devices:

Logos – a plea, an opinion, facts to support reason.
Pathos – emotional empathy, pity, compassion, sadness.
Ethos – the ethics and credibility, the moral of a story.

Each quality has a different language. *Logos* is more reasoned and 'databased'. *Pathos* requires imagery and metaphor. *Ethos* is present to explore the morality, justness and rightness of a story or debate. There are hundreds of rhetorical forms to enhance content, but these three are critical in serving our minds, our hearts and our sense of right and wrong.

The Greeks started a very conscious campaign to deprive women of their voices and their natural ability to structure thoughts by not educating women in rhetoric and by not giving them an opportunity to use and practise their communication.

When Greek civilization fell, it was replaced by a more savage and destructive empire, the Roman Empire – the one that we are really based upon.

The Romans stayed long enough for people to forget that once upon a time women had voices and power. Europe forgot that women could have power, could choose who to marry, could keep their wealth. The women who could remember were outcasts. Healers, only visited in despair. Seers burnt.

Witches waiting on the heath for Macbeth.

13

THE FADING MEMORY OF WOMEN'S POWER

The violent muting of the woman's voice and the deprivation of education and rhetoric for women continued, and in time the 'Fake News' that women had no real voice or intelligence settled into all modern civilizations.

Most men believed it, most women believed it. Science concluded that women's brains were inferior and that difficult ideas would damage them. Women were troublesome and wily, manipulative and – in some cases – the world would be better without them. Except they produced babies.

But, however hard men tried, they couldn't fully silence women, even after they had recruited many women to do the work for them.

Florence Nightingale knew that the tyranny of marriage and the caring for children would have stopped her revolutionary work in healing and nursing.

And then there were the enlightened men. Those who swam against the tide of conformity. The men who knew that their mother, their sister or their best friend was not inferior. The men who found the outspoken, uncowed, well-read and brilliant women attractive, and loved them as equals.

And some of those men championed the women's rights.

When I asked my father at the age of sixteen why my brother was getting a better, more expensive education than me, his reply was casual. 'You're a girl: and girls don't need a good education.'

I knew he was wrong, as I had already encountered an enlightened man at the bottom of a cupboard. *The Complete Works of William Shakespeare.*

If you read the plays cleanly, the women are matching the men in wit and intelligence, and are winning most of the debates. I felt noticed and *known* by Shakespeare; he shone a clear light on the possibility that I could speak, and be heard, as an equal. These women showed more courage than the men in their articulacy to speak truth and power.

These women were not frightened of being disliked by men.

No one knows how or why Shakespeare wrote these women in a way that none had done before in Western civilization. How he recognized the brilliance of women and was outraged by the way they were not free to be equal in law. Why he shows them as equals in marriage even when there was no conceivable way that the law would recognize their equality. It's possible that he was inspired by Elizabeth I – a highly intelligent and educated woman. Or maybe he was married to a brilliant women who took him on and won in wit and debate. He definitely knew women could love as passionately and profoundly as men. He knew that they were called 'mad' when they were filled with grief and rage, and that they deserved justice.

Unlike many of my female colleagues in theatre, I wasn't sent to a great school. It was sufficient, but not demanding, and didn't encourage girls to excel. I was not taught to believe I could compete in the higher echelons of the world.

There were, and are, girls' schools that had a vision of women in leadership roles. Schools where the teachers were often 'spinsters', with a political agenda about the rights of women.

But I self-educated, as thousands of women have done.

By speaking Shakespeare aloud I learnt about ideas and how to think better and more clearly. It was a lonely endeavour, but it was a door into another room.

Thousands of women and less privileged men have learnt the skills taught only to elite men in this way. A curious and ambitious mind can learn this by listening. Listening attentively to a powerful, theatrical debate. Listening to the people you admire when they speak, or to those you know you should speak to, or to those you know you should challenge. And prepare well for those whose presence frightens you: this could mean remembering to stay present in Second Circle with them and to breathe. And preparing aloud, before a meeting, the ideas you know you should speak.

Today, some of the finest speakers and communicators come from societies that are still bardic, the storytellers. People not nailed to the floor by academia, or fearful of getting it wrong. People interested in making an impact with a story.

In most traditions, women have always been the custodians of stories. Stories and information that, before the written word, were crucial to know and remember. Stories about a group's history. The geography of the environment – where water is, or good grazing – and the group's morality and ethical code. The stories were precious, so the storytellers were honoured, and carried when they could no longer walk and keep up with the group. The elders respected and revered.

The nurse in *Romeo and Juliet* knows and guards Juliet's early history. Her parents know nothing of their daughter's childhood. We never learn her name: she is the nurse, a working-class woman in service to a wealthy family. There is no evidence that she can read, but she can remember, and speaks exactly what she knows.

My nanna was only known by me as Nanna until I was fourteen, when I was looking at her marriage certificate.

'Your name is Winifred Edith!'

'My friends call me Winnie.'

I had never heard that name. She was called Nanna by all the people I knew.

The nurse in *Romeo and Juliet* names her lost daughter Susan. Shakespeare knew that the nannas are 'Nanna', and nurses are 'Nurse'. The name disappears inside the job or role when the wealthy employ the working classes.

One of the oldest jokes in theatre – Greek and Roman – is the servant who is brighter than the master or mistress. Sharper, wittier and a better communicator than their expensively educated 'betters'.

If you are clever and around learning and educated speakers, you can easily pick up language and accent. You can see what goes down, and do it better than those in charge. Crucially though, an ability to speak effectively is key.

Maria in *Twelfth Night* eats the expensively educated Sir Andrew Aguecheek for breakfast. She can read and write and has learnt to forge her mistress Olivia's handwriting. She is on the road to betterment; in fact, her whole plot is to dupe another servant so she can marry Sir Toby Belch and become a lady.

In Shakespeare, the highly articulate and intelligent women might only be recognized by men when the woman is disguised as a man. This is a sophisticated mask that allows the man to have a profound and equal conversation with a woman, not knowing she is a woman. This disguise educated men that women can be equal, if not better, than them in mind and voice.

Women have found social mobility by learning to speak and express themselves well, and this expression has disguised their roots.

George Bernard Shaw's Mrs Warren in *Mrs Warren's Profession*, starts as a prostitute at Victoria Station and improves herself to the point of being considered the epitome of a cultivated and sophisticated member of the upper classes. The one thing she does for her own daughter is pay for the best education she can.

Some years ago, I was invited to a party in an apartment on Fifth Avenue in New York. I was informed by my American friends that the apartment belonged to an English lady from the minor aristocracy. It was a beautiful apartment. But when I was introduced to the hostess, I felt a real fear from her. She was all grace and impeccable manners, but was resisting any engagement with me. She had not realized I was a voice and speech teacher until the introduction. From that moment, although it was exquisitely disguised, I was not welcome. Later in the evening we found ourselves alone for a few minutes. The rest of the party was in high hilarity on her extensive balcony.

She looked straight at me and said, 'You know.'

I held her gaze. 'Yes: I know.'

'You know that I am a working-class girl from Birmingham?'

'I didn't know that you're from Birmingham, but I know you have studied your accent superbly.'

'Then how do you know?' All the tension was gone, she was smiling with curiosity.

'It's too perfect.' Exactly how Eliza Doolittle is exposed. 'And I won't tell anyone.'

Another smile. 'Thank you.'

Until her death we would meet and drink champagne, and I learnt some of her remarkable journey in becoming an 'Aristocrat' – 'minor' her own enlightened proviso. A modern day Mrs Warren, in the days before Facebook could expose the path she had taken: a courtesan who had built her own life and wealth, her own way.

Tony Blair's first Labour government had a revolutionary number of women who had been elected into parliament and power. The majority of these women had been educated in the state system and hadn't had the luxury of spoken learning or the study of rhetoric.

I worked with some of them. One of their concerns was this: they were confused by and admired the Conservative MP's ability to be debating a point, be knocked off that point by a question, and ten minutes later, after an intellectual scrum and multiple interruptions, find their way back to the point they had left some time ago. These women had not been taught debate or practised it until they had power.

The Conservatives, women and men, had come from private schools, had studied the classics and had presented in public throughout their schooling and professional lives on a weekly if not daily basis. Spoken learning. They had been trained in forms and structures, and read aloud the classics, which are powerfully structured texts. For instance, if you study Milton's *Paradise Lost*, the text will require you to tell an epic story, then leave it to explore a long simile that relates to the story – maybe ten lines of a diversion – before you return and continue.

This is a simple process but needs practising using voice *and* mind. You practise as if the idea is a journey – you set off on the road, with the beginning of an idea, ready at all times to pause or suspend the thought and the breath should you have to. If you are compelled to take an unexpected diversion, an aggressive interruption from an opponent that requires an immediate response, learn to travel this new path – the answer to your opponent – for as long as is needed. Then you can return with renewed energy to pick up the road and the thought where you left off. It is an embodied sensation that can be felt and experienced and can then be transferred into all your communication. These ambitious, bright women learnt this craft in three sessions and began to control their opponents and debate on equal terms.

In my early teaching I knew that I had a prejudice against a rigid, 'proper' way of speaking. The type of work I had done in elocution classes.

I was sent to elocution lessons to learn to speak with confidence and without hesitation and mumbling. My love of poetry was ignited, but I found speaking out in class just as difficult. I feared the teacher's harsh criticisms. I spoke poetry out aloud in my room at home but froze in public. I wouldn't go to parties as I was scared of the communication required with the other children.

My speech hesitation was laughed at, and I grew petrified when the class was engaged in reading around the room. In fact, we were sight-reading, and as any skilled actors will confirm, this is the hardest thing to do. It's probably one of the top reasons why young people feel like failures when they try to read an important text. I was very shy. Now I realize that this shyness was attached to not being able to make casual conversation. As I have mentioned, I was a serious child and not liked because of that. I hated the elocution classes. I never got it right, whatever right was!

One morning I asked my mother if I had to continue with the classes. Our cleaner, Mrs Dack, was in the kitchen and overheard my complaints. She appeared in the doorway. My mental image of her now as then was of a woman weighed down with the drudgery of life. She walked as though she was dragging a cart through a muddy field.

'I wish I could afford to give my daughters classes like that. It would give them a start in life.'

The passion and clarity of her intervention was so vivid that I went to classes differently and more appreciatively from then on.

I didn't go to a great school but it wasn't a school that taught girls to please men. I had female teaches that encouraged me. They did what they could in the place and time they were teaching in.

Miss Otway taught philosophy to six year olds. She made us learn about poetry, and never suggested that a girl couldn't read a war poem written by a man.

Mrs Breakey, as well as being a fine classist who took the risk of slipping off-course literature to me, saw my curiosity and, I think, my courage in not hanging out with the popular girls. She also knew my messiness had creativity in it, and then was tough and unconditionally caring. She told me my writing was a mess and that no one would read my interesting ideas if it didn't improve. This led me to study italic writing, and through an excruciating period in my fourteenth year I changed the way I wrote. My mother remembered me sitting weeping with frustration for months as I slowly learnt to write clearly and beautifully. It was only later that I realized that the agony I had felt having to write clearly was the same I felt in having to speak clearly. And I still feel it. But both were vital to me in enabling my ability to communicate my ideas.

These women encouraged and supported me, but I knew my mind should be more finely tuned.

Within a week at the Royal Central School I learned that some men believed that women's voices were inferior and were unable to serve a great text. This was the next great challenge that I had to meet.

14

JOHN

Within the first weeks of arriving at The Royal Central School, I knew that neither my mind nor my voice were to be challenged as I had hoped. Actually, the school would challenge me in a much more demanding and testing way – my imagination and vulnerability would be shifted forever.

The ethos of training, then, was to find things out for yourself. You weren't told how to do something, you had to look, think and change without exact instruction. The deep learning I received was through encounters with extraordinarily creative people, and the greatest impact on me was made by a man called John Roberts.

John was a brilliant teacher. He was fearless and refused to make education easy. You had to wrestle with ideas and your craft in his class. But he always made us feel safe, and the mess he made us confront in our processes was creative. He was a wit and a clown. He made demands. Not a sympathetic listener. *Be clear. Use a better word. Communicate better. What do you mean?* Later I found out that his impeccable speech and clarity had been imposed over a working-class Birmingham accent.

My encounter with John was powerful enough, but the people he knew and the circles he entered were beyond belief.

He had no fear sparring with anyone. Great academics who could think and speak brilliantly but had thin voices. Writers, directors, fine artists. Then the actors, passionate and beautifully spoken, but often not sparring with the rationality of the intellectuals. No one had a free passage. No one was untested. No sympathy if you couldn't keep up: interrupt, but it better be worth it. Tell a good story, a good joke. Express an interesting idea and don't sulk if you are attacked.

It was terrifying, but it was what I had waited for. It reminded me of the Greek philosopher, Epicurus: anyone from any class could join the table, eat and drink as long as you contributed something interesting.

John always with humour.

Always with danger.

He tested me and I learnt to test him.

I fell in love.

I married a man twenty-five years older than me. I was twenty-four.

I met my English teacher Mrs Breakey at a bus stop just before the wedding and she smiled.

'Yes, an older man will not be afraid of your intensity.'

John was a charismatic teacher. No one, I fear, will be able to make me laugh as he did. Even my mother – who didn't like him – would laugh until the tears rolled down her face. He and my father would drink and laugh. Drink until neither could stand. They enjoyed each other to the extent that my father took his side when I left the marriage. I never stopped loving John, and I maintained that love and engagement until he died in 2015.

He was drowning and I chose not to drown with him, but that is not this story.

He was the first man to say to me: 'You know more about Shakespeare than I do.' This to a twenty-five year old, from a man who had acted in the company that became the Royal Shakespeare Company (RSC). A man trained by Michel Saint-Denis and who had taught Shakespeare for years. It was not flattery, or said with anger or envy; it was just a clear recognition of my knowledge and insight.

Equally, the first man to ask me to choose the wine at a meal! To younger readers I have to say that it was not uncommon for many men to choose the wine for women in restaurants up until the 1980s. They even ordered the food they wanted you to eat.

He listened to my opinions, handed me books I should read and was delighted with insights he had missed. And he generously gave me access to his circle of friends and colleagues. Through them I learnt about language, ideas and a passion for the life of an artist. People a young woman could only dream about meeting. I was fast-tracked into a world that I still live in.

Part of the power and presence these encounters and friendships gave was that I never knew who I was going to meet. He never prepared me, and simply trusted that I could and would survive. Sometimes only just.

His contacts went back to the fifties. I was seamlessly introduced to an elite world of actors, writers, directors, designers and other worlds of painters and eccentrics. Old ladies and gentlemen who had been part of the Bloomsbury Group. He didn't explain who they were, I had to figure it out. He was loved by many of them and made them laugh, and they welcomed me. It was a new and wonderful and dangerous world. Always with cocktails and fine food.

John had an otherness about him. He had passionate connections to women and men. He wasn't in a box and I began to realize that he was the centre of a group of artists who, in the parlance of the time, swung every way. It wasn't an easy place to be as a suburban, young woman. It was a creative one, but I was left wondering what 'conventional' lines were being crossed. Where were the boundaries? And who is hunting who? Who benefits? I know now that it was the men.

Married men who were gay and had families, children and wives; those women with a haunted look in their eyes always wondering *Is he interested in the young girls? Or the boys?*

I was taken into the middle of families and groups that all had strong connections to John, and I never fully understood what those connections were. It was made very clear that to enquire would be unsophisticated and worst of all 'suburban'. Beautiful, rich, successful well-mannered men and women who seemed to have long and intimate relationships with him.

My childhood desire for otherness was granted, and it wasn't a place that was comfortable. I had not been trained to have the kind of explicit conversations about unconventional relationships I should have had with John. When asked he never lied, but saw no reason to swear to change his life or his passions.

These were not politically correct times, and the debates, wit and discussions I entered were fierce and passionate with blood on the floor. Words fuelling, piercing and igniting ideas about life, wit and ethics. I was the youngest there and knew I was out of my depth, and John wasn't going to come to my rescue. I had to pull my weight or I had no right to be there. And he wanted me there.

The first strategy I instinctively employed was to stay extremely attentive: be still and listen. Taking it all in and knowing what was going on before I opened my mouth, and if I was going to speak, to be informed about the subject, audible, clear and passionate. No hesitation, use accurate language and don't be offended if you are interrupted, but get back in and stand your ground. Find a right to be there.

In my observations I quickly realized that there was no forgiveness, no sympathy, for inadequate speaking. In a strange way this displayed an equality. The ideas, the communication and the game was what was important.

There was the sixties brigade who would mock 'Get on with it, Sweetie!' to the rambler. 'Can't hear you!' to the mumbler. 'Do you really mean that word? Well learn how to pronounce it darling!' 'Don't go shrill!' – to the women. 'Don't bray!' – to the men. 'Bit dull!' – to the dull.

Very harsh and not for the weak-hearted. John was in the centre, mocking the intellectuals, who would mock him back. Mocking the rambling academics who would mock him back. John winning through wit and laughter.

I only realized later that a lesser me would have crumbled. It was an exhilarating test. I hadn't been to Oxbridge and experienced the gladiatorial debates there, but even that was mocked. No one got away with anything not communicated effectively. It was cruel but always truthful. A clown – John – worked through truth, however harsh or appropriately cruel, and he could turn on a sixpence, which meant he could go too far and a ruckus would kick off.

Now I don't believe this baptism of fire or initiation was fair, but somewhere along the road, the truth about how effectively we communicate has to be told. We are not fair to those we want to help unless we tell the truth, even if it's hard or painful to hear. As long as any negative note is tempered with tenderness and a practical correction. It is not fair to not teach craft, not fair not to raise the bar, not fair to not challenge intelligence.

In company you have to be present if only listening and appreciating. My father understood that, and it was a gift he gave to me. He took me to events, knowing that I knew when to wag my tail and bark – but not roll over and show my tummy! But his business associates and city connections were not witty or well-informed sparrers! I could bark without finesse. I would have to up my game and I would have to suffer John's contempt if I was not clear and apt. Any note given to me by John was for me to figure out how to achieve.

As I started to teach, I felt that this was unfair, and it reminded me of myself as a child; being criticized without being given the guidance I needed to make the change. I started to gives notes to students about their voice, speech or language, only if I could help them to change it. A correction needs clear, physical instruction.

This wasn't John's way. John's way was the way I had been taught at school. This was of its time, just as the notes that I was given as a child about my speech were not accompanied by the exercises to help me improve. It's a hard balance.

I sometimes imagine transporting my ambitious, young students back to the tables in the 1970s. John holding court and the rest rolling up the sleeves of their voices, wit and language to go into combat. It was a test, and until you are tested you don't know where you have to work. Brilliant and ambitious young people do not want to be stroked, but lovingly challenged – at the right time and in a safe space.

Just a small taste of the world I entered in my mid-twenties.

Meals with Terence Rattigan and Tennessee Williams.

Coming home after work to find Ava Gardner in the apartment drinking a cocktail and talking about 'Frankie'.

Katherine Hepburn talking about *Measure for Measure*. John teasing her. She had rehearsed in slacks and found it impossible to move when the heavy dress of her costume was put on. John, getting excited, 'I *told* you to wear a practice skirt!' Laughter. 'And then the staircase! You couldn't get down the staircase in your costume.'

The last survivors from the Bloomsbury Group describing Evelyn Waugh swinging on a chandelier, and Vita's garden.

Ten years of an education.

One of the most brilliant men I met was the director and writer, Ronald Eyre. Not only a theatre and opera director, but he had just made the BBC documentary *The Long Search*, which I had loved. Ron was a profound thinker, visionary, and also a TV and theatre director.

Two years after I left John, I was coaching in Stratford, Ontario in Canada. Ron Eyre had come there to direct *The Government Inspector* and we reconnected. One night I girded my loins and asked Ron whether he remembered meeting me with John. He looked at me with a wry smile. And then repeated – almost verbatim – a conversation we had had about Mozart six years previously. These words were a gift that brought me to a place of trust in my own ability to deliver interesting ideas. I had passed the test that John trusted I could pass.

From then on, Ron was my close friend and mentor until his death in 1994. His wisdom still visits me most days: a mixture of the most uncompromising passion for the truth, which could be fearful, and an unconditional love when you had the courage to stay with any truth he showed you.

15
SCARLS

In 1976 I met John Scarlett – Scarls to all who knew him – through John. He was in his mid-sixties, I was twenty-three. A tall, impressive looking man. Dressed in quality clothes. Erudite, charming, kind – and an alcoholic.

He had been connected to the Royal Opera House, the Royal Ballet and The Old Vic as a touring manager. He'd come from a wealthy family who had disowned him: there was a suspicion he had been imprisoned for homosexuality – I didn't pry, so I never knew the truth.

By the time I met him he was living in a squalid, basement flat in Englefield Road, Islington, with an ancient bath and a toilet in an outside hut.

He was at the bottom of his heap.

His drunken bouts had lost him most of his friends, but when he was coherent, his wit and wisdom were outstanding. He had worked with, and was at some point loved by, great dancers and opera singers, and actors, which is how John knew him.

On first meeting him I sensed that he knew something of me, and I could feel his love and curiosity. We met a year before his descent became uncontainable. Seamlessly, I became his last carer.

I was teaching, performing in theatre and education, and cleaning houses, but once a day I would go to his flat. I would feed and wash Scarls and do the pointless hunt for the hidden bottles of cheap sherry – never finding them all, and amazed that he could get up the street to Essex Road to stock up at the off-licence.

Then the master class began.

I had loved the contralto Kathleen Ferrier since my childhood. Beside Scarls's battered record player was a stack of records. Later, I recognized they were only women's voices. I showed my delight at the Kathleen Ferrier and he became excited.

'Put it on!'

Her voice in Gluck's *Orfeo ed Euridice* filled the grim, basement room with its half-boarded window and battered furniture. Scarls lying on his bed, newly washed, newly fed, eyes shut and in bliss. We listened. At the end he opened his eyes and talked about Kathleen – he had met her – but mostly he talked about her voice, her breath support, her phrasing, the placing of the sound, the connection to the words. The acting through the music.

So the routine was set. I knew emotionally but only realized intellectually later that he was giving me vital insights to his life in opera.

Every day we would listen to opera or recitals, and Scarls would then explain to me the craft we had heard, how the magic had worked: and the magic became greater and more magical when Scarls talked about it. 'The woman's voice is my bliss. The woman's voice breaks my heart.' That remark opened *my* heart in a way I hadn't felt before: *The Woman's Voice*.

His collection was vast and wide. The records and some decent clothes were all that were left from his remarkable life. His favourites – all singers he had worked with or had met – Maria Callas, Victoria de los Ángeles and Jessye Norman, as well as Kathleen Ferrier.

My master class continued through the autumn of 1976 until the summer of 1977.

It was thrilling. I had never heard the voice spoken about in the way that Scarls did. I hadn't worked with singers or opera yet, but I knew I was being taught something so relevant and important, and it was a special gift.

When I told John, he couldn't believe that Scarls knew about the voice, so it was for me, only for me: all his memories of the women's voice, his meditations on this most heightened use of the voice and its connection to music and words.

The master classes finished abruptly.

I arrived slightly late from cleaning a house in Hampstead. I hated being late. I let myself in and called out, 'Scarls!' No answer. Then I couldn't find him. Had he gone out to the off-licence? He had been mugged a couple of times doing so, and I had had to mop the blood up from his bald head as he never wanted an ambulance or the police involved. I was about to go up to Essex Road when I stopped, and rushed to the shed with the old claw-footed bath and the toilet I couldn't ever get to look clean.

There he was.

In the bath holding on to the side – just – for life.

'You're late.'

'So sorry.'

'Get me out, get me out!'

Scarls was more than six foot but now skinny ('Belsen, my dear, Belsen' was his exclamation about his body). I rolled up my sleeves and leaned over the high sides of the ancient bath. The water was cold, he had been there for some time then, and it was the colour of blood.

My arms found their way under his knees and the lower part of the back. In a fraction of a second I knew I couldn't lift him.

Scarls felt my failure in that second.

'Patsy, you have to lift me.'

My shoulders released, my knees bent, I felt my feet fully on the floor, but mostly I felt my breath go deeply into the lower part of my abdomen and I felt intense love for and from Scarls.

At that moment, he let go of the side of the bath, his arms were around my neck and he was out, in my arms, as light as a feather.

That moment has remained one of the most powerful experiences of intensity and love I have ever felt.

I got him onto the bed, dried him, dressed him and made a cup of strong, sweet tea.

'Scarls, why the fuck did you have a bath without me?'

'Oh you know, I thought it might cure me, wash it all away, Luv.'

I was about to make a quip when his eyes turned sharp and serious.

'Patsy, call 999. It's about time an ambulance came for me.'

While we waited I played Victoria de los Ángeles singing *Bailero*. *Chants d'Auvergne*. Scarls's last request.

He shut his eyes and listened. The ambulance came and he was off to St Bartholomew's Hospital. I followed and when I found where he was the nurse asked me for more details to put on his admission form.

I didn't know if he had a next of kin. My name was put down. Religion: I knew he was Roman Catholic (RC), but I also knew he had hated the priests who had taught him at his RC boarding school. They had been cruel, and probably with hindsight, he had been abused.

My fear and middle class need to answer questions posed by authority led me to tell her he was RC.

It took Scarls ten days to die. He shut his eyes when he didn't want to engage, but I knew when he wasn't asleep. He remained vital and witty when he had energy, and sent me on bizarre errands that for a moment he believed would cure him. One was to search for a fresh pineapple. 'Not the tinned shit.' This was nearly impossible to find in London in 1977. Or I didn't know where to look and didn't have the money. Eventually I found a scraggy one and brought it in triumph to the ward. He was asleep, so I left it on his bedside table. The next day it was gone and Scarls hadn't seen it, but he was agitated about something else.

'A fucking priest came and tried to give me the last rites or wanted some bollocking confession.'

I was so ashamed. I didn't dare to tell him that I had given his religion on admittance.

On cue the priest reappeared in the ward. Scarls hissed, 'Get rid of him, Patsy, get rid of him!' He shut his eyes and feigned sleep. The priest moved towards the bed. I stood up and moved to meet him and block his way. I was polite but said clearly that I knew that Scarls didn't want a priest. This one was not going to be a pushover. I stood firm. He got angry with me. I remembered the Rev from the Library. A woman has sacred authority too.

'Leave him alone. I made the mistake of telling the hospital that he was a Catholic. He didn't want people to know. He hated the priests who taught him. They were cruel. Please go.'

And he went. Scarls's eyes were still closed in mock sleep. I sat down. He opened his eyes and looked at me. He had heard that I had created the priest mess in the first place. Silence. Then, 'That told him. Well done, Patsy. You told him.' Then the Scarls eye twinkle. Was this going to be my punishment? 'I need a wet shave. Do me a favour Luv – go and find a razor, a shaving brush, shaving soap; take John's. And while you are at it, take some of his most expensive cologne. Vetiver I think it is. Off you go and come back soon.'

I had been fired from my cleaning job in these last days as I was attending on Scarls, and my teaching was re-scheduled as required. I went home and took a new razor and brush, some soap and the cologne. Scarls was waiting for me when I got back to the ward.

'That took you time.'

'I was fast.'

'Get on with it.'

It hadn't occurred to me that I was to do the shaving. 'I can't shave you! I have never shaved a man.'

'Don't be so stupid, Patsy, get some warm water and shave me.'

And I did. I got a good lather going and I did a pretty good job. Scarls was still and trusted me completely. When I had finished he was pleased and then, 'And now the cologne.'

I dabbed some on his face and neck. 'No, no, no – I want all of it on me and everywhere. I want to be cleanly shaven and smelling wonderfully.'

The whole bottle was used.

When he was satisfied that there was no Vetiver left he said, 'Thank you, that's better. Thank you, Patsy.' Then he shut his eyes – the signal for me to go – and I left.

Scarls died that night.

Cleanly shaven and smelling wonderfully.

Three months later I was asked to teach my first opera singers. And because of Scarls's masterclasses, I could.

16
FOCUSING ON VOICE

Everything I had ever obsessed about at home, at school, in the street, everywhere, came into a focus, for me, around voice.

The power, the tone and the language of women came down to their physical voice, and all the stories I loved concerned a woman finding her voice. All the stories of the loss of voice, the silencing of women: this was what had always upset me. And all the stories of how women had found their voices and their stories: this was what moved me.

At Royal Central School I had great voice, dialect, text and speech teachers, and great movement and acting teachers. When I could, I attended lectures in the speech therapy course. I wanted to understand the anatomy of the voice and the voice's disorders.

But something was missing.

The voice work was sound, but not muscular.

There was imaginative and improvised vocal work, but there was no application of craft or the required repetition to make muscular work organic. When I questioned staff about this, they didn't cast any light on my worries, although there was sympathy. It was later that I found out why there was a fear of craft in the work.

Ten years before I trained there, there had been a devastating split at the Royal Central School. Some staff and students broke with the traditions of craft, and particularly the voice work done by the principal, Gwynneth Thurburn, a renowned classical voice teacher. She had taught all of the great leading actors of the forties and fifties – Olivier, Richardson, Redgrave, Ashcroft. The 1963 breakaway group deemed her classes to be an issue. The muscular and epic vocal range and clarity of her work was mocked because it was felt that it was creating an inauthentic sound. An 'actor's' voice. The new plays needed a gentler and more nuanced work that had no prescribed routine or exacting craft.

The split broke Gwynneth's heart, and many people told me that when she and I met in the mid-seventies, it was a shock to them that she decided to talk about voice work to me. I innocently asked her questions and she answered with relish. We had a powerful and loving exchange on all things voice: for me, a rich, transforming and delightful encounter.

Cicely Berry continued the voice work at the Royal Central School in a less crafted and more naturalistic way. Poetry was at the heart of the training – clear speech was there from Margot Braund – but sustained stretching and releasing of the voice was not.

We would lie on the floor, it seemed for hours, gently breathing and humming. We drifted off. We fell asleep. This gentle approach was a necessary re-balancing of voice work, countering the vigorous breath and voice work of the 'old school'.

I knew something was missing.

Understanding what was missing has taken years to specifically comprehend. Re-balancing vocal training has taken me much thought and practise.

It's not a coincidence that the split happened when working-class actors had begun to train. In the fifties, working-class playwrights had forged a new theatre and different voices and accents were required, which was wonderful. The great, classical actors of the forties and fifties had more released and less blocked voices. Partly because of class, and the spoken education that public school and upper-middle-class students had, including using their voices in large spaces on a regular basis. And partly because of the fact that many actors had gone through the war. They had been in the services, fought, flew spitfires, served in the Fire Service like my mother, had nursed the wounded, and had therefore come to theatre later and older. They weren't so vocally hesitant or as held. After what they had gone through, a bit of vocal release was not a difficulty. Harsh events around them had unblocked their voices. When they learnt craft from Gwynneth Thurburn, it enhanced and focused these naturally released voices, not inhibiting them.

In the sixties, the students began to be different and needed a different approach. Their voices were not so free. Craft, which is placed onto voices that are not released, sounds odd and not organic. They were young and had a different perspective from students training in the forties and fifties. Not so entitled, not so at home with power.

As I have taught through major changes in education, I realize that you have to teach in the time you live in, and that the teaching has to re-balance the world that the student has come from. The truth is the same, but the process of finding truth does change. There are many doors into the same room. Truth, clarity and authenticity – but the door chosen is determined by the student and the time we live in.

You cannot build a muscular voice until your natural voice has been re-discovered.

Craft in the sixties was often being imposed on top of a disconnected, unnatural voice. Power without connection. Craft was relegated to history and a less physical routine put in place. The relaxed approach did and still does create connected speech, but hasn't got much power and can be inaudible and unclear, particularly in theatres.

In the seventies it was clear to me that my voice and those of the other women in the year were more disconnected than the men's. We had been more conditioned into bad habits and physical reduction. As I've said before, it takes more time and work to improve a woman's voice.

Six years after leaving the Royal Central School, I, very nervously, announced my first main house warm up for the RSC at The Barbican.

First into the room was Dame Peggy Ashcroft. She looked directly into my eyes and said firmly: 'I hope you are not going to warm us up lying on the floor. We don't like that.'

After that I couldn't lie the actors down – I was going to, it was the format I had been trained to do – but her remark gave me another piece of the jigsaw, and context.

An actor needs to be fully engaged to act well. Lying on the floor deactivates them and creates too much relaxation. This amazing actor needed to have her breath and voice prepared for a large space. She had decades on stage and knew exactly what she needed. Great theatre actors do know what they need.

It occurred to me in that moment that I was there to serve the actors: not entertain them and do the work on my terms, but prepare them in a way that would help them deliver the play and engage the audience.

When I graduated from the Royal Central School I was asked to join the voice department there. I was honoured but also hesitant.

I had started to teach supply in tough London schools and in prisons. I was teaching voice tutorials to non-actors. Mostly, desperately incoherent speakers, who had no apparent pathological speech defects but had deep-seated issues that were reflected in their speech. Something was wrong with them and I was often out of my depth. Working with women who were under threat at work, being bullied and who hoped that learning to answer back might help. I was teaching the embodiment of the voice, by applying standing, breathing and speaking aloud exercises to all my students, before they tried to work it out silently. It's the delivery. And they noticed, as I did, that *they* understood what they said better when they spoke it aloud. We were discovering ancient wisdom. This was exactly what the Ancient Greek and Roman educators knew. The work was suddenly relevant – this wasn't humming on the floor.

The job at the Royal Central School beckoned. I hesitated. The money was good. But I knew there was a part of my training that wasn't complete. I knew I had to seek something else.

I had started to hear about the classical voice work done at the Webber Douglas Academy by a teacher called Sheila Moriarty.

I wrote the only letter requesting work that I have ever sent to Webber Douglas.

I got a job there with Sheila.

The amazing, brilliant and terrifying, Sheila Moriarty.

Sheila was a classical teacher of the 'Old School'! She hated the modern voice work and was closely connected to opera and classical singers. Her work was the complete opposite to the work at the Royal Central School. It was muscular, extreme, sequenced – and the foundation was relentless repetition. Hours and hours of repetition.

I became her apprentice. I taught twenty-one hours a week for her. I was teaching in six other institutions and also cleaned houses to make ends meet.

In fine apprentice style, I drove her around in my battered, little car, got her lunch and would hang on every word she said. Sheila knew a lot, and I knew, even if I didn't agree with her on all subjects, that what she knew was essential and was being lost in the voice world.

As I grew in confidence and courage, I began to formulate questions about the work and her processes – which she in the 1970s had traced back 150 years.

Questioning was dangerous, as she could be acerbically dismissive of my ignorance, particularly as I had trained at the Royal Central School. This was my first encounter with a consistently powerful and entrenched view that there is only one way.

Her comments about the students were harsh and yet had truth in them. I was used to these remarks, as that was how I had been taught, and wounded. It was at this time I realized I didn't want to teach with the sharpened dagger of brilliant one-line put downs. I also noticed that the female students were mocked more than the men. By the male *and* female teachers.

This is what I learnt and did for Sheila.

Seven groups, two classes a week of one-and-a-half hours each – twenty-one hours.

In each one-and-a-half hour class, I was to accurately repeat a sequence of energetic body, breath, voice, range, resonance and speech exercises. When I say accurately, I mean accurately! Not only was the exercise to be realized in its exact form, but each exercise was to take a certain time. If Sheila entered the studio at ten minutes past the hour and I wasn't on the correct exercise – maybe thirty seconds out – or if I was teaching it wrongly, she reprimanded me in front of the students.

For the first year I hated this, but somewhere in me I knew I was gaining knowledge. It was so different from the Royal Central School way.

Then, in the second year, something began to change in me as I taught her repetitions.

Something deeper occurred and I could begin to link not only the work I was doing, but to understand something about the work I hadn't done.

I started to find love and relief in repetition. Something I now know great performers and sports stars have experienced. A safety, and the possibility of effortlessly unleashing presence and power.

A few years after I left Sheila and was teaching at Guildhall, I discovered a wonderful gift from her and what she had made me do: mid class I realized I could exercise a group freely, change the order to serve them, doing what they needed, but always find my way back to the journey of the sequence.

I had had enough teaching and repeating structure to improvise! My thought was 'I don't know what I'll do next, but if I stay present with the students, I'll know what's needed and therefore I'll *know* what to do next.'

The magic of having craft, knowing and knowing, knowing.

I thanked Sheila that day and I still thank her most days of my life for making me learn the power of repetition, and the humility required to honour the form and security that comes through craft.

A few years ago I was approached while standing on the subway platform of 96th Street, New York. It was a student I had taught at Webber Douglas, now a successful Broadway actor. I was ashamed of how robotic my classes must have been. He kindly said they weren't, and he told me that he knew that Sheila used to check on me. Something, he had observed, that she didn't do to her male staff.

Was she checking on me because I was a woman, or because I was inexperienced or not good? As these questions crossed my mind, the ex-student gave me half an answer.

'The male teachers were old fashioned and didn't teach well – I still do the work you taught.'

Was Sheila one of those women who trusted men, honoured them and would not challenge them? Whatever, her diligence over my craft development has been critical in my teaching life.

I also taught poetry at Webber Douglas without any interference from Sheila, which was wonderful, and after a few years I realized that the structures of teaching voice craft applied to teaching the structures of poetic form. The building blocks of voice-craft transformed into an authentic connection, with form and content making a seamless union.

Like Scarls, Sheila also introduced me to the world of opera, and I was her attentive assistant at opera rehearsals.

Under her strict instructions, I learnt how to warm up a singing voice, Scarls's happy ghost standing beside me.

The staff room at Webber Douglas was dominated by Sheila. The teaching staff, mainly women, the directors, mainly men, who we were all there to serve and honour. The teaching was chaotic, eccentric, often brilliant and consistently dangerous.

The staff qualifications were long experience and long careers – this didn't apply to me, although I did have a qualification! Coached by John, I sat still and listened and learnt.

There was much laughter, vicious wit and camping about.

The discussion about the women students was, I suppose, normal then, but appalling.

'Who's going to tell her she's too fat?'

'With a face like that, how does she think she can play Cleopatra?'

The drama school sexual playpen applied equally to the female and male students. As I got more confidence, I began to object. This was noted but not challenged, although conversations stopped when I walked into the room, and within a few months I didn't sit in the staff room anymore. I had other jobs that I went to, so that became easier to do; however, one of my breakthrough moments in my work happened in that staff room.

I overheard a conversation as I collected my poetry books – vicious voices from the cabal, discussing one shy but talented student.

'What is that silly girl doing here?' Laughter.

'I know darling: she hasn't got IT.'

'Never will have . . . I've given up teaching her.'

Pause.

'Charlie's got IT.'

'In buckets he has IT.'

With a full, camp delivery: 'You can say that again!'

Roars of laughter.

The whole class was marked on their 'IT' factor, or lack of it.

As I walked to Gloucester Road underground station, I wrestled with the 'IT' factor.

My first reaction was that the girl they said had no IT, did have IT. I had seen her ITness, and through that, her talent. They were wrong. I still feel ashamed that I didn't defend her. But I was only twenty-five myself that day.

But what is IT? Their assumption was that IT could not be taught. But could it?

What are the signs of IT? In the body, breath, voice, speech, eyes, ears, mind, heart? How could I help her embody and consistently find her 'ITness'?

That moment in late 1978 put me onto the long, and still being travelled path, of the Three Circles of Energy.

It took me at least twenty years to have a coherent set of exercises to release the IT in us all. My first full understanding was that we are all, mostly, born with IT. IT is our natural presence and survival mode, our curiosity. *To be or not to be, that is the question*. To be fully present, we have to be fully engaged – for example to the world outside us, or specifically connected to a person or place. We are fully alive. That full aliveness has a powerful charismatic effect on all around us. The energy is palpable. We are in a balanced place. Full presence, which I now call Second Circle. Balance between giving out and taking in. Speaking and listening.

In teaching I realized that you can see and embody this balance. In the body, in the breath and in the voice.

The 'IT' is us. I used to call it *The state of readiness*. Now I call it the Second Circle.

I used to call First Circle *Denial*. This is when our energy falls back into our bodies. You can see this in the body slumped, hunched and depressed, the breath shallow, the voice underpowered, the eyes disconnected. Take not give.

The Third Circle – what I used to call *Bluff* – is when the energy is forced out, pushed. Chest up, rigid and stuck body, voice too loud, breath too apparent. Give not take.

I was an innocent teacher starting this exploration, but I immediately and sadly realized that First Circle energy is found more in women than in men. Closing down their bodies, hunching over. Not taking space. Maybe listening but not sharing.

Third Circle is more apparent in men. Pushing out, forcing, bluffing, shouting, not listening. Chest puffed. Taking space.

Both First and Third positions de-sensitize you and put you in danger.

Second Circle is the energy of full awareness and survival, and the need to be aware of others, manners and our humanity.

We are all moving more and more into First Circle. Urbanization and the technology that we believe connects us to the world is closing us down into deeper, lonelier bubbles.

Third Circle is now wrongly mistaken as Alpha. The tensions held in Third Circle create a shell that has its own loneliness and disconnect. The hollow people, the narcissists.

Things I hadn't understood began to gather some sense. I began to understand how power embodied itself – in body, breath, voice. In language, and in how our energy predicted how the world would change us.

It seemed then, and it still seems now, that without finding our natural physical and vocal power, no one, male or female, can fully transform or be taken seriously and recognized fully.

17
HANDMAIDENS

For years, women in all work situations have been expected to know everything about their work and to share it selflessly with men. To move the company forward, and accept that at best they will be cherished and loved, though often gently mocked. Stroked but not allowed a killing. Able to join the lads for drinks, as long as you remain fearlessly loyal to the boss. Hide his mistakes. Be the gatekeeper. Not complain and never expect promotion or leadership. Without these women most organizations would fail within weeks, if not days.

Some women are content to be needed and useful and never in the limelight, but they really haven't had a choice.

The list of brilliant, pioneering women whose work was stolen and owned by men is slowly being revealed.

This pattern was clear all through the first twenty-five years of my career. At The Royal Central School, female teachers retreated with grace when a male teacher got up to work – even when the man was less experienced and knowledgeable. I saw female teachers taking more time to pacify male students, therefore serving them differently and with more respect.

I watched this in my early teaching and early coaching.

I had no problem being a handmaiden when I was learning and knew that the person leading the room was more knowledgeable and more experienced than I was. It became harder when my work and ideas were taken and owned without any recognition coming my way. My intellect and experience used without even a nod of thanks or acknowledgement.

I am still coaching female leaders who are treated as handmaidens not only by superiors, but by their male employees who can't carry their own workload and expect these women to save them. They exhaust themselves by serving the men they work with, one way or another. It is very, very hard to break the habit of centuries. They find themselves doing a double job.

I was twenty-five years into my career when I felt I had served too many who knew too little.

One day, years before, I had asked Sheila, 'Why do you think most voice teachers are women?'

'Men won't serve as handmaidens. And women are more sensitive.' This was the first time I'd heard the word used in this way, and I was uncomfortable. I hadn't thought of myself as a handmaiden. I believed in service. In education, your service is to the pupil or student, but I sensed she didn't mean that. I knew our philosophies differed and this was too painful a wound to open.

She must have seen my hesitation.

'We are handmaidens to the director or conductor. We do his will. Our power is in the tutorials. There, away from his view, we can do as we please.'

This, of course, is how women have got by for millennia.

But, there was another way to serve.

Cicely Berry (Cis) took the work into the centre of the company. She didn't work alone with the actors, but with the full company. She changed the work, and the dynamics of the work. Years later I asked her the same question. 'Why are most voice teachers women?'

'The directors don't want a man in the room,' she said. 'Too intimidating for them.'

'Are we handmaidens then, serving the directors?'

'No, we serve the text.'

Yes, that's right. That's what Shakespeare wants from his actors and we help the actors.

1980

The RSC was moving to the Barbican Centre as its London base and was to have a connection with the Guildhall School of Music and Drama. Cicely Berry and Trevor Nunn were looking for a Head of Department for Voice at the Guildhall who would look after the London company's voice work. There had never been a voice job like this. All the voice teachers were chatting about it.

I felt very strongly that I was not qualified for the job, so I didn't apply. I was twenty-seven. There was too much I didn't understand about the work. I knew I was still in apprenticeship. Voice, text and theatre. I had only begun to join up the dots. I was coaching theatre in the provinces and some West End shows but not at the level of the RSC.

Weeks after the first mention of the job, Cicely Berry phoned and asked to meet me. We met at the Aldwych Theatre and chatted. I had worked with her as a student, but I didn't think that she remembered me.

We talked about Gwynneth Thurburn. I think she heard my respect and love for Thurbie and she smiled. I talked about Sheila and the classical work I was doing. I deliberately told her that under Sheila, I had to teach the ancient breath techniques that Cis hated.

Silence. *So put your cards on the table.*

'Given my own freedom, I wouldn't teach like that. I had to do them when I was a child so I know how hard it is, particularly for women.' Many of the techniques taught were designed for a man's body and voice.

Cis looked at me askance, but I continued.

'I've adapted Sheila's techniques so that they work for women as well. This breath-work does give muscle and capacity to the voice.' There, I had said it. Probably lost the job. Her eyes twinkled with mischief. The warm-up call came over the tannoy for the company of *Nicholas Nickleby*.

'Come and do a warm up, Darling, warm up the company.'

'*Bloody hell*,' I thought. My whole career has been like this, in at the deep end. But I always walk into the flames. I warmed up the company. A sequence of body, breath, voice and speech exercises. Later, I would realize that to successfully warm anyone up is one of the hardest things to do.

Cis watched but didn't seem interested. At the end: 'That's alright, Darling.' We parted at the stage door. What was that about? I was dazed and confused.

Three days later I was invited to attend an interview for the job at the Guildhall and RSC. I told John. He toasted me. Toasting was one of his favourite things to do.

The evening after I'd heard I'd got the interview, I met him and the rest of the staff at their favourite table in the Swiss Cottage Pub. G&Ts

all round, and the talk was of the RSC and Guildhall appointment. John kicked me under the table, his not so subtle way of telling me to keep my mouth shut.

Ten minutes into the first interview with Cis and the key Guildhall staff I thought, 'I could do this job. I might be in with a chance.' At this interview I met the acting director of the drama department, Gill Cadell: one of the most magnificent, direct, generous, compassionate, tough and witty leaders I have ever met. She knew what she didn't know and let you do the things you did know. She didn't know how to teach, but respected those who did, and this is exemplary leadership. Gill was a rare species, so I am everlastingly grateful to have met her early in my career as a bright and clear, female role model.

Gill understood that you have to know how to teach, or heal, or build a rocket, not just see the blueprint and think you know. Leaders with no practical appreciation of the work have taken a sledgehammer to some of the greatest organizations in the world.

I got a second interview, and this time I met Trevor Nunn. He didn't say much, but listened. I was left very uncertain about how he felt about me. But soon after this interview and before I knew if I would get the job at the Barbican or not, he was giving me freelance work.

One of the things you have to accept is that highly talented, powerful people sometimes might not overtly praise you, but can display their appreciation by giving you work.

I was offered the job on my third interview.

The excitement and fear were equally balanced. I had never led anything except a class – I now know that leading a department is very similar to leading a class well. The stakes are different, but the processes remarkably the same. And the job is always to make the people you are leading feel safe.

I had never taken a student consecutively through three years of training. I had taught first and second years at Webber Douglas and third years at the Arts Education. I had worked on one show at a time in the commercial sector of theatre and small, fringe companies.

Sitting quietly that evening after John had gone to bed – a lot of toasting – I meditated on the enormity and responsibility I had accepted. I knew that it would take at least four years before I knew what I was doing. The journey of the student from day one to the end. Actually it was more like twelve years!

I knew I had to develop an ensemble. I knew there had to be an ethos that was student based, not based on the whims of individual teachers doing their own thing. Students should be given time to develop, feel safe and grow with their peers and themselves.

There was a common practice in all drama schools then, that you take in more students than you need and throw a third out at the end of the first year. A financial scoop. I was trained with that threat.

I passionately believed this was anathema to the education of a student. In the first year of training you are asking them to strip away their habits and be free and creative – impossible to do if you have an axe hanging over your head. This would have to change.

The last Head of Voice only allowed students into the school if they spoke 'properly', that is with 'received pronunciation'. So ridiculous and wrong. No diversity among the students. All white and mostly middle class. Webber Douglas had a ground-breaking policy of fully training black actors for classical roles – this was rare.

Gill Cadell, back at The Guildhall, was clear and supportive but very sure that my job was to sort out the teaching mess and create a systematic craft training in voice, body and acting. 'You are the first salaried member of staff, you know teaching, get on with it and mind the budget.' In other words you are paid to lead, so lead.

'Remember,' said John, 'that the deal, the *contract* is with the students, and they have to learn to have an honourable contract with the audience. You are responsible for the well-being of the student and what and how they learn, and you are responsible via the student to the state of British theatre.'

Here are some snapshots of the situation I was in:

- There was a teacher who would lock the studio door with all the year inside. Lights out. Demand they took off their clothes and spend an hour and a half rolling around with each other. He was also naked and in his seventies. The students called it Group Grope and Gill wasn't aware it was happening.

- The poetry teacher whose idea of teaching poetry was to dress up in Victorian clothes – bonnet, corset, an apron and carrying a trowel in a trug. She would then perform Thomas Hardy poems.

- The teacher of improvisation who would create storytelling and acrobatic acts that would mostly end in simulated anal sex.

I had to fire people.

Gill supported me; the principal, John Hosier, supported me; but it is hard to fire people. Leadership is messy if your vision for an educational honesty is being undermined.

Without doubt some students didn't want to work. They wanted to grope, fall asleep in class, not be challenged, giggle at a woman with a trug and a bonnet, eat cake before a dance class provided by the teacher – anything to avoid the work. I needed to shake them out of this. But it didn't always go right: the brilliant voice/radio coach I appointed: CV amazing, but he drank and would be in a stupor by the afternoon. Bugger.

But then I did get one appointment superbly right.

Head of Movement – Sue Lefton. Sue is one of the greatest movement teachers for actors in the world. She had been at The Royal Central School before me, studied under Litz Pisk and the famous French movement coach, Lecoq. Seeing Sue teach for the first time, I felt I had come home. Maybe the ethos of The Royal Central School and Lecoq was partially the reason, but it was much more. She was working through her body and the students' bodies with a deep understanding of how everything connects. She was further down the path than I was, but we were both seeking release through dedication. Knowing so you don't have to show you know. Connection to time, space, history, politics all in one movement or sound. Somewhere that exists but you might never get there!

From the first time we worked together we bonded, and that too has got deeper.

Sue had been taught by John, and through all his mess she knew his brilliance. She was and is a home to me. We can laugh and talk about handmaidens. How the charlatans use their handmaidens. The directors who are brilliant, and the ones that are there by luck. Those who do not have the humility to admit what they don't know or what they have learnt from you.

Here is the charlatan routine that Sue and I experienced and bonded over:

'Darling Sue, just teach them that baroque dance you know' (one that has taken Sue ten years to learn deeply). 'I would do it myself but I haven't got the time.'

'Darling Patsy, just get the company clear and audible. I would do it myself if I had the time.'

It is the same for the handmaidens in all organizations.

To the PA who has done all the research on a twentieth of the pay: 'Just tell me how this takeover will work. I have to tell the board.'

The good leaders at least acknowledge your contribution!

It was with Sue that I recognized the root of the word 'maiden'. We are supposed to be virgins. Dedicated fully to our masters. We laughed at the absurdity, but it is harshly real. Male directors that want the full and complete attention of the actors. Jealous of partners of either sex. Angry when they have affairs in the company and not with them. Teachers, angry and jealous when their favourites have relationships in the group.

Theatre

From 1980–2006 I was working most days in the theatre.

In 1990, Richard Eyre asked me to create a Voice Department at the RNT. The wrench with Cis was hard, but she understood that I should create and lead the RNT Company. Within these twenty-six years I worked successfully with most of the major theatre companies in the world. I served the play and enabled actors to serve the play. I stood between the play and the actor, and tried to join them up. Stood between the actor and the director, the designer, the lighting designer, the sound designer.

Coaching is different from teaching.

I tried to enable and what I learnt to do was negotiate. I learnt diplomacy. When to be silent, when to speak – and if you speak, everything you say must be important. You can't waste time.

I learnt that in a creative process everyone is important. Every cog needs attention and acknowledgement. Everything matters.

I learned that everyone is frightened most of the time. Frightened of failure in public. Frightened of success. Frightened of humiliation. Frightened of adoration. Worth and worthlessness trotting beside everyone.

My job was to absorb as much as I could, dissipate the ugly mess and heighten the generous acts of creativity. One of the reasons theatre is so formal is that the formality contains all this mess. The actor takes the approval or disapproval of the audience, so they are on the front line and my initial concern is for them. Many find the influence and power of a famous director daunting, so I am still the one who has to be the go-between. Directors don't necessarily know about acting: some of their acting notes are interesting but unactable, so they require interpreting. The young, unknown director might arouse the ire of the seasoned actor. All their years of being downtrodden finally unleashed on decent, innocent directors. So, then I have to defend the director! At the same time I have to say to designers that the costume is too tight and the actor can't breathe.

I occasionally have to tell the producer that the set that is being designed is so acoustically dead that there is nothing the actor can do to be heard – that if they want the work to be audible, they must change the set.

The lighting needs more light on the actor's face – if we can't see the actor's face they can't be heard.

And then to actors: 'You threw your wig down last night after the show and it was damaged. The wig maker was up all night fixing it. Did you know that wig makers train longer than actors? It's her craft and her artistry that you destroyed in your frustration.' Or, 'The sound desk can't set levels in the technical rehearsals until you speak with performance energy. Don't mutter. They are creating the sound for the show.'

I need a good relationship with the stage managers. They find space for my calls and arrange warm ups. They are critical to a coach.

I realized I had to make contact with the front of house staff to really know whether there were audibility complaints, so I offered voice classes for them. After all, sometimes they have to make announcements.

Hard, but the bottom line is that you have to give notes that people don't want to hear and then have some skill in changing that note. You can't be critical without a solution. I have to give unwelcome notes to actors with compassion and help. I have been asked to give notes that the director is too frightened of giving. Mostly I have survived. I have had to remove other coaches from the rehearsal room when they have been insensitive to the actor's or director's process.

Thanks to Sheila's work, the old actors knew I understood their craft and we trotted along nicely together. A mutual respect. Young coaches were their favourite targets. Lambs into the lion's den!

I learnt to work in a complex network with highly talented individuals, all with things to lose and all being poorly paid. Very few make any serious money from theatre. When things go wrong someone is shouted at by a fraught director, playwright or conductor.

Sometimes it is me and sometimes I shout back.

This is what I have learnt: in general, highly talented individuals will recognize very quickly whether you can do the job or not. The more talented, the more secure, the less paranoid in a very paranoid world.

The problems I have had are with less talented individuals. The fear of being found out is often a destructive force that lands on any expert in the room.

Actors, the doers, are more open to negotiation than directors.

I have wonderful, working relationships with writers. They all want their words heard and are glad that someone is striving to enable that.

I have had great working relationships with most great directors. The men are more direct as to what they want and what they don't like. Any problems are more discussable but there is less praise. Now, it's clear that this so often comes from male privilege – especially if they are white men.

The great, women directors are more generous with their praise and talk around their problems before they conclude. This can annoy actors.

Women have to be *better*. The young women I worked with in 1980 were much better than the men, but were not given the breaks they should have had. They're still working, but not at the level they should be – and not with the respect and prestige they should be enjoying. Women actors are generally better. There are more roles for men to practise getting better. Most women would give a lot for the supporting role a man moans about.

In twenty-six years I opened an average of forty-five shows a year, led six warm ups a week, and sometimes three in one evening for three different casts.

I was a handmaiden and a good one, but like all handmaidens, endured the fact they don't want to pay you much and they definitely don't want you to lead on your terms.

But, never underestimate what you learn as a handmaiden. Diplomacy, how to negotiate throughout the building and beyond. You do things that the leaders won't, or more accurately, can't do. As you get better at this service the last thing the organization wants to do is promote you. You are the hub, the trouble shooter, the diplomat. Generally, I knew more about the work than those I served did.

The apprenticeship was over.

18
BREAKING FREE – GOING DEEPER – DEMANDING MORE

In the medieval structure of apprenticeship, an apprentice was expected to learn their craft in seven years. They would then make a masterpiece, judged by masters, and then, if the piece passed, they would be a master in their chosen trade. One of the markers of knowing your craft is that the skill and embodied processes that support artistry become organic.

For those who use their voice professionally, such as actors, this means that delivery, presence, body, breath, voice and speech are so known that although they might need constant attention in the form of a warm up, the craft supports their artistry to tell a story well.

An actor cannot interpret or thrill an audience until their craft is organic. They might be audible and clear, but the audience cannot be transported to another world if they can observe an actor's craft. It is the same with a musician, dancer, writer or leader. And because craft is only embedded and organic when there is sufficient dedication, application and repetition, it is not achievable unless the student is seeking excellence and works hard to improve their craft.

And the constant paradox is that a master works hard in the search for perfection, knowing it is never reached. Maybe for a moment but not in a sustained way.

It took me more than twenty years to finish my apprenticeship. Long before that it occurred to me that I had not finished a stage of my vocation. I was termed a master but knew it wasn't true.

Maybe I am 'slow of study', but it took a long time for me to know I could hold a space and embody work through well-explained exercises that were efficiently structured. Then to diagnose a student's habit and it's source in the body and breath. I knew that I had to break free from the rigid and repetitive patterns of teaching and coaching. And although I didn't know where it would take me or the work, I knew something had to be deepened and something had to be demanded of me and my teaching.

And at the bottom of my heart was a sense of disappointment and failure.

Women's voices in the 1990s were not getting better, they were getting worse. More locked into their bodies, thinner, or, more pushed and aggressive, making them hard to listen to. Not all, but many women didn't think it mattered that their voices were ineffectual. What mattered was how they looked, not how they sounded. They were scrupulous about their appearance but careless about their voices and their stories, and passionless about their rights. The mentioning of feminism could produce a smirk on their faces rather like my father's smirk. It seemed that twenty-five years of equality had damaged, not released, the women's voice.

I had time to reflect upon and analyse this disturbing pattern.

No, it wasn't true that all women were lazy and passionless. But, there were women who could *afford* to be lazy and passionless. Women who thought that they were heard, although it was clear they weren't. White, Western, educated women. My tribe. I wasn't reaching the sensibilities of privileged women. Women who felt safe and didn't feel the need to change, like the cat in its cosy Primrose Hill house. I began to re-remember Nanna's clear, blue eyes focused on me whenever I showed her any sign of middle-class decadence. But there were other visitations from my teaching. Ghosts of women I had met throughout my twenty-five years of apprenticeship.

They started to haunt me.

Hamlet begins with men awaiting the appearance of a ghost.

It was that opening that had gripped my nine-year-old imagination. Something was rotten in the state of Denmark.

The ghosts awaiting me when I dared to wait for them were women who were not white, educated or rooted in Western civilization. Their knowledge and haunting was deeper and more important for me to understand. More powerful than my father's footprints on my shoulders. These ghosts were trying to awaken me. What were they saying? And why was it so upsetting and challenging?

They were handing me pieces of a puzzle to ponder.

Like the glass in the shop windows haunting Tom in *The Glass Menagerie*. Tom had run away from his responsibility. My childhood puzzle was around fairness and the responsibility of power, and now these re-remembered encounters were attacking this Western, educated woman's knowledge – or lack of it.

Interestingly, these ghosts came from early career encounters before I had status and was maybe considered more challengeable; and they were clearly reminding me that Western women were naïve and obsessed with the cosmetic and youth. That we thought that explanation instead of experience could change us, unaware how dangerous the world really was for women. That we were losing our deep intuition and ignoring the gifts of fear. In short, our Western, unenlightened feminism was dominant, and our ignorance was putting non-Western women at risk. Our power was seated in privilege and veered towards decadence: at best we were stupid.

The only comfort I had when visited by these vivid memories was that I had really learned something from these women. It had just taken me a long time to understand. They were kind to me.

I first noticed this when I taught prostitutes in Holloway prison, or through Clean Break Theatre company. They learned voice and language skills quickly and gratefully and would often take time to explain darker truths to me. They were patient and kind and the knowledge they shared was not to shock me but to warn me. *Don't think you're in control or safe.* The unpredictable violent turn a prostitute so often has to experience and survive. It's always a possibility: *Don't think it can't land on you!* In the 1970s, Peter Sutcliffe, the Yorkshire Ripper, was only deemed dangerous when he started to kill women who were not sex workers. I hitch-hiked through Europe in the 1970s but had courage because I was stupid and naïve. These conversations with my prison students triggered memories of events that could have resulted in my death. There but for the grace of God go I.

There were other memories.

In a Canadian voice workshop the audience heard the sacred Inuit throat singing. The stories women tell by singing in their throat as it is too cold to sing through their mouths.

At the end of the session the throat singers were bombarded by 'how to' questions – 'How do you do it?' 'Where's your tongue when you do it?' 'Do you ever take breath through the mouth?' Members of the audience wanted a facile explanation of a sacred, deeply worked craft that was outside Western vocal experience.

I could see the Inuit women getting upset and refusing to answer stupid questions, and as they refused to answer, some of the voice teachers, there to enjoy an elite experience, got angry. They had paid to come to the session, so they believed they had a right to know. One of them got up and stated directly – 'I've paid for this: so tell me.'

I found myself standing and speaking. I don't remember what I said but it was about how those questions were not fair. To me, trying to capture in a few moments a sacred and ancient tradition was just crass, and because I knew some of these teachers were singers, I threw in a question of my own to them. 'Would you ask Pavarotti how he does it?'

The session ended, and as we shuffled out, one of the Inuit elders touched me on the back. I turned and she held my hands firmly and looked right into me. There was appreciation in her look, but there was also the challenge: *These unanswerable questions come from your tradition. Deal with it. It's your problem.*

Are we that enlightened? Are we the custodians of all knowledge? Should we be teaching? A fortunate gift in my life has been that, while teaching around the world, people from the indigenous population who have often attended my scheduled workshops have then invited me to work with them in their communities. I have had similar encounters with female elders from the Navajo, Hopi and Pueblo people. Always the openness, and always the challenge: *What are you going to do about it?* when Westerners want a shortcut to their knowledge.

One of the most thrilling and educational experiences I've ever had was being invited to attend the sacred songline singing of indigenous Australians. This happened because I had been teaching a group of students in a community centre just outside Perth. At first they were all quiet, withdrawn – stuck in First Circle. Over the days I worked with them, they began to reveal their full and effortless vocal power. When they noticed my delight and shock, they asked their elders if they could invite me to the corroboree. It was only as I watched that I understood how honoured I was – that this was an act of them trusting my sensibility. But again, always with the shadow thrown on me: *This is what your tradition is destroying.*

Then, in Poland, the Romany storyteller, most of her family lost in Auschwitz. At the first night's banquet, after the wine had flowed, she turned on all the English-speaking voice teachers. We were, she blazed, smug, self-satisfied and knew nothing about the cost of storytelling. It was a magnificent, terrifying, passionate tirade. We met a Eumenide. Most of the party left but my dear friend from India, Alaknanda Samarth and I stayed, and gradually the tirade dropped a few notches in intensity. She watched me and I listened. This phase was about our obsession with perfection, getting it right, shallowness, decadence. It was hard and true.

The next day the keynotes started.

She attended them all, and her questions to each presenter were harsh. My keynote was given on the last day. I always engage audiences by doing exercises, not only explaining. And afterwards, she approached me.

'So!' She hugged me. 'You do know something real!' Still smiling, she took a heavy gold ring off her finger and gave it to me. I still have it.

My first, long teaching tour in India in 1986 changed me profoundly.

I had been asked by the British Council and the Indian government to teach teachers and actors throughout the subcontinent. One workshop was held in a leper colony that was situated beside a speech school.

The helplessness of teaching in a leper colony, but doing my best! I was trying to teach people who had lost most of their face and therefore their ability to communicate. It was a sledgehammer to my heart. So many life-changing experiences and many of them not beautiful but extremely disturbing.

After I had left the colony, during another workshop, I particularly provoked the rage of a group of women towards my 'Western stupidity'. My aim had been to try to teach them to be centred, open and powerfully revealed. My naiveté was an anathema to them. They demanded to be taught without any men in the room. This was arranged.

There were sixty women. I was at the front waiting to begin the class, the door barred against men.

Their spokeswoman, traces of anger at my stupidity still in her voice, stepped forth.

'We understand what you're trying to do. We understand that, as you put it, if we stand as we do, feet close together, eyes and head looking down, we cannot breathe for power and our voices will sound weak and often inaudible.

But Miss Rodenburg, what you are asking us to do is natural and right, but you must understand what the consequences will be for us if we do this. This is a revolutionary act and it could be punished by rape, disfigurement or death.'

Before I could answer another woman took the floor.

'In any case you Western women pretend you are men and think that is power!'

Immediately she and several others did a crude but effective imitation of a Western woman posturing and strutting like a man. Swaggering, chest pulled up, and a pushed, aggressive-sounding voice.

Laughing with delight, I joined in with that particular walk, and the ice was broken as we all gave a display of Third Circle bluff.

And they were right: many Western women seeking power did this cosmetic display of male hollow bravado in the 1980s. Wearing padded shoulders and sleek, well-cut imitations of men's suits, some women thought they had found power. With a cosmetic disguise of masculine dress and habits, with nothing real at its core. A show of power with no real substance.

'I don't want that,' I said. 'I want you centred, breathing and powering your voice naturally. Real power, not show power.'

The spokeswoman said, 'We know. But please remember that we have known all of these things for thousands of years. It is in our culture. You are bringing us nothing new. But this knowledge is supposed to be barred from women here. We understand being centred and we don't wear those stupid shoes you tend to. We know the importance of full contact with the earth.

So, please, re-teach us to stand, breathe, and power our voices, which is our natural right, and then, show us how to stand as men want us to stand; small and meek without eye contact. But so we have the choice to keep our power even if we choose not to be attacked.' And that's what we started to do. We refound their natural power and then let the habit be a choice that kept them safe but not permanently reduced.

The stance that we worked on that day is the same stance that any cruel oppressor demands from those perceived as inferior. The stance is imposed through fear and pettiness.

Servants, slaves, women and children have all been placed in this reduced, physical position.

A cowering. A bowing. A caging of the 'underdog'! But, an underdog that the master knows – maybe only instinctively – has huge power and intelligence.

A theatre audience knows that long before the actors speak, their present energy signals status and power. If an audience sees the curtain rise at the beginning of the show and a character is standing on an empty stage in First Circle – feet together, body closed down, head looking down – the immediate assumption is that this is a servant or an inferior.

This process was easy for me to teach, as any good actor can go from a strong, centred stance to one showing an inferior servant: but with the power and presence underneath the disguise of inferiority. It's an everyday transformation happening in any good, rehearsal room with skilled actors.

Since my visit to India, my connections with some of their finest artists grew and I had powerful exchanges with remarkable women who taught me.

The renowned director, Veenapani Chawla, came and stayed with me in my house for a few months, and I introduced her to the breath work used by Western actors. She introduced me to Indian techniques.

Veenapani came with me to the Guildhall and was allowed to move around classes.

One evening she returned to my Camberwell house in a rage.

She had observed a male teacher teaching Chi breath – an ancient, sacred, Eastern breath tradition that she had studied for years.

Part of our teaching exchange had been me teaching her English swear words at her request.

Now she let them organically rip.

'How the *fuck* can a Western man teach Chi breath when he has only done a workshop or two?! When I questioned him he quoted the books he had read! Don't you fucking Westerners understand that you have to do the work, not read about it?! It is so damned stupid! And why are you letting him teach what he doesn't know? It takes twenty years of *doing* what he has *read* about!'

Of course she was right. She made me understand the practical meaning of embodiment, deeply owning knowledge in your body.

Embodiment can only be achieved through the repetition of craft work.

A few years later, Neela Bhaghat, a renowned Hindu sacred singer, came to study with me. During one session she explained that a sacred song cycle that she sang had only become within the reach of her voice in her sixties. This was partly to do with the craft work but also because of the degree of wisdom and experience her body, mind, heart and spirit held and needed to sing. This reminded me of an early Renaissance model of artistry. Through craft, an artist can one day reach a place of grace, divine intervention. So Western civilization did know: but it has been forgotten.

In 1994 I was teaching with the National Theatre Studio in South Africa, and spent time in Soweto. I had been invited by a Zulu actress who I met at the Market Theatre Johannesburg, to work with some of her friends there.

It is true that every person a teacher teaches, teaches the teacher. And these Zulu women certainly taught me more than I taught them.

They, too, requested the work without men being present.

As the class began, the women explained that Zulu is a calling language. Free and released to carry over space. A series of calls burst from the group as they demonstrated.

Then the challenge.

'Before the whites came, we believed our vocal folds were in our stomachs.'

They watched me take that in and waited. The image was so wonderful, because we do power our voice from the stomach, and therefore what they were saying had absolute truth in it but not for a Western 'scientific' mind.

The power of the voice starts in the breath, and the deeper the breath the stronger the voice. So, scientifically the voice is powered from the stomach but the sound starts in the throat.

Without the breath there can be no voice. Without the hand, without fingers striking the guitar strings, the guitar is silent. The Zulu women said to me, 'So we know where the voice really starts.' And I replied 'Yes; and that understanding was lost for many years in the teaching of voice in the West.' And they laughed.

This remark took me back to my early teaching, and some of the work I did with ENT doctors. In the 1980s, I worked with clinically damaged voices, alongside Garfield Davies and Robert Sataloff. Both these surgeons knew that merely working on the throat section of the voice did not solve the problem. Only by understanding the physical breath from the stomach can you save a damaged voice.

Very apparently and quickly, working with these women on Shakespeare – which they loved and knew – I realized they had none of the physical and vocal habits that Western women have. They were fully present. Fully in their bodies, and could release their free and natural voices. And, crucially, they could understand the full connection in voice production that many Westerners don't. I didn't need to explain the whole physical connection of voice work. No system in their body was divided.

They didn't need craft work. They had never lost their natural voices in the way that Western groups had and had needed to refind. Societies living in a world completely dependent on technology have lost their human connection and, often, their ability to survive without that technology – although a decadent sense of safety can encourage the feeling that they are in control. These women walked across Soweto, always navigating danger and the chance of rape. 'We know,' they said. 'We walk in danger, we have to stay in ourselves, we know it is dangerous to be a woman. But it is also our community that keeps us present and alert.'

They had to be in Second Circle as they walked over rough ground, as they physically laboured and talked. Told stories in a community of listening, seeing and speaking. They told me these things and looked at me askance when I thought about them. Always, always on the verge of gently teasing me.

'Teaching over many years I have seen the presence, body and voice of my students dwindle,' I said.

No reaction.

'I have often thought that Shakespeare's actors . . . ' The group got interested. ' . . . Wouldn't have needed this basic work. A Londoner in Shakespeare's time would have been able to use their bodies, voices and presence. Walking through constant danger, on rough ground.'

Laughter. 'Like us!' Another voice from the back of the room: 'We are more like Shakespeare than you!' More laughter.

I could only agree.

They began to warm to the idea of Western women's disconnection from their physical power. 'You Western women do a sway walk.' Someone added, 'We do this hip-sway walk when we want to get a man.' All of them did their version of the walk to attract a man.

Laughter.

'We choose, we don't do it all the time.'

There it was: *the choice*. You can't work or walk efficiently if you sway your hips all the time. You can't carry goods on your head – we picked up our bags and tried it. It's impossible to walk and sway without wasting energy and feeling physically off-balance.

At the end of our time together the spokeswoman who had steered the group, and me, gave me a compliment:

'You are the first white person who has laughed with us, not at us.' She knew her Shakespeare. 'Shylock,' she said: 'If you prick us do we not bleed? If you tickle us do we not laugh?'

'Yes,' I agreed. 'We tickled each other.'

Tokyo 1992

If the fashion in the West is for women to bluff and to adopt a lower vocal pitch to imitate men, then the Japanese female actors pitch their voices up. As do the corporate women.

I was asked to teach corporate women and female actors without men in the room. They believed they would be mocked if their voices weren't pitched up and 'whining' – their description.

But first, I started teaching the all-male Kabuki company and have been told – although I don't know whether this is true – that I was the first woman to teach them.

They bowed and I bowed back. I felt their well-hidden distaste at being taught by a woman. The first few moments standing in front of those very powerful and impressive men was terrible. Their request was simple and urgent. The actors use a fully stretched vocal range and many were losing and damaging their voices. They didn't know how to remedy this physical abuse. Many were desperate, as the thought of not having control over your voice when you are in front of an audience is horrendous.

I could see why the damage was happening immediately. Their chests were held, and the breath not fully connected, particularly when they made lower notes. Their physical bracing and lack of breath was trapping their larynxes in their necks and creating tensions. I worked on upper chest and jaw release, on the low breath supporting their voice, and things began to improve. They felt the difference and began to trust the craft I was teaching. We had a creative time together. They began to open their throats and no longer feel discomfort or pain.

It was a peculiar irony that the women were being asked to speak too high and the men too low without full breath.

When I taught the women, I released them into their natural lower pitch by doing almost the same routine as the men. Open throat, lower breath, the larynx dropped and their natural free voice emerged.

The more startling insight came days later.

Every night I was taken out by the production company to share lavish meals with actors, designers and theatre lovers.

All parts in the Kabuki are played by men, and they are often members of the same family. You can witness a thirty-year-old man playing an eighteen-year-old lover opposite his eighty-year-old father playing a sixteen-year-old girl. The men playing women adopt a high pitched, sing-song voice: a parody of a silly girl!

In an unguarded moment over dinner I pondered whether the men adopt the voice of women that they want to hear. Not a true woman's voice. This thought was strongly challenging to them, and I apologized. Later, at 5.00 am, the phone in my hotel room rang. It was a man I had barely noticed at the evening meal. He turned out to be a theatre historian. He explained that my comment had upset him and that he had spent hours reading accounts of audience members attending the Kabuki in the seventeenth and eighteenth centuries. He apologized to me. Courtesans had visited the theatre to learn to speak as men wanted them to sound – high and sing-song and without a full tone, a 'girl's voice'. The presumption was that was how men wanted women to sound.

That was the insight I gave my women and after the shock we all laughed. It seemed so obvious! They were rewarded for their 'whines' and punished for their full vocal power.

It was a ridiculous mistake I had made in not working with Western women in groups free of men. I had a vague sense that these women knew that the men around them were blatantly mocking any notion of equality. But then, I had not fully computed the impact of a male presence on women who believed they had their rights. I began to realize that in the groups I coached, many men had become skilled at wearing the disguise of being a liberated man with high morals and enlightenment.

And it wasn't consistent that young women didn't care. I began to see that working class and BAME students were more ambitious to change their voices and to put in the work to change the way they communicated. This was before the terrible exposures of the 2000s. How theatre, the BBC, charities, the Church, the Law and Healing contained some of the worst perpetrators of the abuse of male sexual power against women and children.

I was working in companies that had managed to hide and disguise their misogyny and had got away with it for decades. An irony began to present itself to me. I knew from a very early age that every woman understood male power. We had lived through thousands of years understanding through experience how devastating it could be, and we had devised extremely sophisticated disguises to survive their power.

Suddenly I knew that educated men had watched female disguises for as many years and knew now how to adopt them to beguile women. And these disguises were extremely effective in the spaces that were proclaimed as safe for women.

Male rage at our equality could thrive behind the disguise of being a good guy, making women feel safe, as their power was not violently but softly eroded. Women of my age and older were continually shocked by the lack of skill shown by some of the younger actresses. One great dame of the theatre was appalled by the inaudibility of a young woman she was playing opposite. She came to me after trying to help the younger woman. She had been mocked: 'I don't take notes from you.'

I went to the male director and requested a voice tutorial to work with the young film star. The director smirked. 'But she looks gorgeous, leave her alone, I love what she's doing.'

'She's inaudible!' I insisted. 'And the other actors on stage can't hear their cues.'

'The audience just want to see her.' He shrugged and walked away.

So, I thought, she doesn't have to have a voice or power, just be 'gorgeous'.

I was eventually allowed to make her audible when the complaints about not being able to hear her flowed into the theatre. The hidden misogyny had become dangerous in these 'safe places' and would be exposed eighteen years later when the full backlash against women's power was exposed.

In the meantime I had started to work in places that were 'civilized' in setting but savage to women, and these women, outside the arts, knew that there was no safe place in this world.

Wall Street. A bank.

Fourteen investment bankers in the room. Thirteen men. One woman.

The usual bully was stretched out in his chair with the smirk hovering. I was just managing to keep him in check.

As people got up to work he showed interest but gave no feedback or compliments.

The woman got up. She stood in front of the group and took a breath to start.

At that moment he shouted out. 'Crack a smile, babe, you look better when you smile.'

There was shock in the room. Some men laughed. The woman was rightly agitated but was courageous enough to not do what he hoped she would do. Laugh at herself, smile or even flirt with him.

I looked at him and asked 'Why didn't you ask your other colleagues to crack a smile before they started?'

'Oh fuck,' he replied, 'You're not a fucking feminist are you?'

I ignored that and repeated my question to him. The woman, shaken, joined in on my side – defending herself and repeating the question.

At this point some of the men agreed that he was an 'asshole'.

The woman then spoke with power and clarity and in essence said that he was a sexist bully, and that no one had ever tackled him before and no one in the bank had ever addressed his attacks on women.

In the sessions I had with her after the event she proved that with basic craft she could maintain her power and dignity. The other vivid realization was that most of the men in the group knew he was vile and they could express the obvious once it had been called.

This event is not unique in my teaching.

In the 2000s, a full tide of women from a non-theatre background sought my help. They were certain that they were not safe, that men had just adopted masks to hide their contempt for their new power.

I started to run courses just for women. I could progress their voices faster without any judgement from men in the room and – their observation – any competition from other women to gain male approval over each other.

They could express profound ideas without being mocked or having to laugh and belittle themselves. They could take their time without feeling that they were going to be interrupted. They could tell stories about their failures and their shame in failure without any male smirking in the room.

They could find their power with their vulnerability – the highest display of authority any leader shows. They could begin to marry the fineness of their minds with empathy and compassion. Or train their minds to focus and structure ideas alongside their humanity.

These workshops were devised by me for women. I wasn't doing them in a corporate setting. The idea of that was ridiculed by any HR department I discussed it with.

The argument against it was simple. Women have to work with men, so they should be allowed to sink or swim. But, I countered, it's harder for women to find the basic power of their presence and voice. It is harder to release and harder for them to trust. Wall Street is more savage for women. The incident that fully focused my mind was not uncommon, but it hit my heart hard.

The ideal circumstance for an actor in the theatre to be safe and creative, is what we call the ensemble. It's agreed between the actors that the ensemble is there to serve the play not the individual. It is a safe and equal place that presents the opportunity for deep and meaningful work to happen. This is an ideal, but if it has been experienced, it will never be forgotten and will give an actor the resilience to stay present and released. The same started to be true about these women, their courage grew in the safe place, and they reported it transferred to the unsafe male-dominated places.

This was echoed by women outside the arts world, who worked in spaces that were dominated by men who were not disguised as ' good guys'. Women leaders from the military, engineering, the law, police and trucking.

These women also invited me into their male arenas to teach and experience the unfiltered men.

I was challenged mainly if they had read about my theatre and film work. They had had coaching from out-of-work actors, and one description that stuck was 'They have all the sizzle but no steak.' This from a bullish New York banker who grudgingly apologized at the end of the session. 'I've learned some useful stuff.'

'Steak.'

'Yes, some steak – not that touchy feely shit.'

Whenever I work with these embattled women who know they are not considered equal and are not safe, I remember the Hopi elder who told me 'We move on when the living gets too easy, so we never forget how to survive.'

19

2006: MOVING ON – THE REVOLUTION OF THRIVING, NOT JUST SURVIVING

I had journeyed an apprenticeship of thirty years, and had moved on away from work that kept me contained. This resulted in me having time to meditate on the state of my work.

I very quickly realized a hard truth: women were still struggling to be heard.

In schools, in theatre, in business. Western women's voices were more masked and held, their presence more impaired than it had been in the 1970s.

A male backlash was intensifying.

Many women were reporting that the men they worked with, or were in a relationship with, and who had initially been supportive of their growth, were now turning on them. Particularly when these women started to significantly succeed. It was as if *male* furies were gathering. Not in the spirit of the ancient female Eumenides for justice – but in a spirit of spite, to deny women's equality and push them back into their cages. From some men, the outrage of 'How dare you believe you are equal, let alone think you can lead?!'

Was it that these men thought that female equality was an experiment from the 1970s that was bound, and now due, to fail?

Women started to feel the familiar patriarchal response when any part of men's power is threatened. The usual violence employed to stop their voices and stories. Literal violence, or simply the threat of it. The *thump*, until we concede. In some cases this has broken and erased women. But all through history, some have also known how to mask themselves, to hide and preserve their power.

Now in the twenty-first century, they were not backing down, so the violence was accelerating.

The 1980s and 1990s were a period of educational cuts that exacerbated the problem. Quick fixes became acceptable, instead of deep learning. Craft was once again being mocked (and still is, in some establishments), women's voices were getting worse because more and more of these quick-fix plasters were rapidly stuck over our historic tensions and masks, creating more layers of impediments to our ability to communicate.

I knew I had to take women back to their full natural presence and voice, and, vitally, not promise that it could be done without struggle and work. 'The short cuts,' as one female executive said to me, 'haven't worked.'

Nor had the tricks that many coaches were teaching, and still are. The most common trick I hear is 'Tell a joke – make them laugh,' which doesn't work for women.

A very brilliant and witty woman told me this story: 'In the late 1980s, I was very young, still in my twenties, and was thrilled to have got the high powered job I'd always wanted. I attempted to break the ice with my new, nearly all male colleagues by doing what came naturally to me – I tried to make them laugh. But the atmosphere remained distinctly chilly. After a few days of this, one of the less aggressive men took me aside and explained, "Look, men don't want you to be funny. They don't want *you* to make *them* laugh. MEN want to be funny – they want to be the ones making each other, or women, laugh. I'm telling you this to help you." This explained why I'd been astonished to hear my jokes, which had met with stony silence when I told them, getting roars of laughter when one of the men said the same thing, verbatim, minutes later. The theft had felt so brazen to me, but now I got it.'

I had to take time and encourage the women I worked with to take time and go back, to refind their full presence and voice. To take time to reconnect to their stories.

It was at this moment that I realized that for a woman to take time to work on themselves and with themselves it is a revolutionary act.

1 It is a revolutionary act for a woman to demand time and space around themselves.

2 It is a revolutionary act for a woman to take the time to take a breath and look at an audience before they begin.

3 It is a revolutionary act to slow down and not rush.

Women have to fight for space and time around themselves, but in many of the organizations I worked in, there was a mantra that women were good at multitasking. This allowed men to 'admit' they couldn't multitask, and therefore have to pass on their 'extra' work to their female peers. Often with a smile, 'You do this *so* much better than I do.' We now know that when you multitask you might do a lot of things, but none of them very well. Women's excellence was being compromised. They were being held back.

One of the first women who did this work with me and refound herself, said,

'I feel I have come home, to a place I remember from my childhood – it *is* my authentic presence.' She had abandoned her Third Circle tension and reconnected with her natural power. She realized, 'It's not a failure to take time, or discover what you can't do. You just have to work at it.

The work, works.'

The three main strategies that women adopt to display power are placed on top of their natural presence and voice, and strangle their voices more. These strategies are:

1 Imitating the worst habits of men by moving into Third Circle. Bluffing power. Pushing their voices down, and often straining them. Interrupting and adopting an aggressive tone. This strategy has some success, but never leads to significant power. In their early career, when they were younger, they were tolerated by men and even flirted with, but this didn't consolidate their place: they weren't subsequently trusted or helped into power.

2 Other women chose to absent themselves and moved into First Circle. They got on with their work, gained huge and deep knowledge, and with a quiet dignity, waited to be noticed. And

sometimes they were. Decent male leaders promoted them for their knowledge, even though they had no voice. They were then sent to me, to help find their voice.

3   The third strategy is to 'look really good' and seek the impossible perfection of a fantasy woman who doesn't exist. Tight and revealing clothes, impossibly high heels, and layers of make-up. The female entourage around President Trump demonstrated the pinnacle of this strategy. Cosmetically-honed, so encased and constrained in their shell, that they, grown women, sound like eight-year-old girls. This unthreatening 'little girl's voice', used around men who have no respect for women, means that their intelligence might be heard. Most women dealing with that kind of man have used this strategy to survive.

No women should be blamed, or should blame themselves, if they use these masks to defend themselves. And you maintain your power on your own terms, if you do it by choice.

I knew then, and know even better now, that it is your full authentic presence and voice that will give you authority, your equality and leadership recognized. I had to make a decision twenty years ago not to dilute the truth to women. I had thought that by doing so, I was being supportive. But it was something I didn't do with men of the equivalent status. The truth is harder for women: they haven't come from an equal place – their starting line is so much further back.

Harder still is that you have to take some responsibility if you are not heard or taken seriously. And the truth I have to tell around this is that you are facing unsympathetic listeners: some men do not want to hear you. There will be sacrifices that many men don't face when you speak out with your full power. You will be punished in a way that men wouldn't be.

The female CEO of an engineering company had discovered this truth and told me: 'Speak out. No one will speak out for you. No one will defend you until you do. Men defend other men before they're asked, but not the women.'

As I started to tell the truth to women, I experienced their relief, not their anger. I had forgotten to transfer knowledge that was in my bones from all my years in theatre. Fully present theatre actors know when they aren't heard, are boring or the audience is unsympathetic. They know when their voice is alienating an audience.

As I told the truth to these women who worked in savage, male-dominated organizations and companies – women from banking, engineering, the military, the police force – they expressed their rage to me as though for the first time.

They began to speak about the meanness and naked cruelty of most of the men around them. They told their stories about choices. To join these men in being mean, and in doing this desensitize themselves in Third Circle – the sacrifice being that their vulnerability and intuition and wisdom closed down. But when they did simple work with me, the change was rapid. We talked about being too driven and too focused, and they knew it had hurt them.

In these classes we allowed ourselves to be messy and unstructured, so I resisted giving them strict sequences and lists. I let them play with their presence and voice. The tears were of relief as they came back into their presence and their bodies. Not the tears of rage and pain when they had first come to me. These armoured women were hungry for knowledge and to be in balance.

We talked about balance as a mixture between power and vulnerability. A give and take of energy. A readiness in body, mind and heart. Of getting things right and sometimes wrong. The moment of being centred but active. Standing on and at the centre of the see-saw. Always ready to go in any direction.

This is hard if there are men waiting for you to get something wrong. The female COO of an international bank told me, 'Men will always find and voice every fault of a woman leader, but rarely voice the faults of male leaders.'

They knew that Third Circle energy is insensitive to the world but it gets you through the mockery and delivers fast results. Some women knew that this bluff had even cut them off from their families.

These women have to wear a uniform. Granted, a very expensive one. They have to power dress in elegant and mostly restrictive clothes. Often tight fitting and with encumbering accessories. Corporate clothes for women are another burden on their voices. I've had to help men speak with dress collars, a cummerbund and chains of office, but this is nothing compared to what is expected of women.

I helped the women make small adjustments to their clothes, which enabled them to breathe and power their voice better.

However open they had been to my suggestions, so often their last stand was to do with their shoes. High heels have become the source of power for so many women. It's a quick fix of what feels to them to be authority. They give height, and display legs to a great advantage.

Most knew that in a formal presentation heels made them shuffle and wobble, and stopped them stabilizing themselves through the floor. This consequently meant that they had to lift up the chest, making them breathless and their voice go up in pitch. They had learned to believe that the effect of the high heels mattered more than their voice.

I explained that when your feet are not on the floor, the breath gets locked, as does the larynx, which diminishes range and forces the voice to go up and become shrill and not come down again. The knees lock, the stomach gets held in, the shoulders tight or pulled round, and the sternum depressed or pulled up too high.

I told them this story.

In the seventies my husband John took me down to the Royal Vauxhall Tavern, one of the best known and oldest gay pubs in London. He promised me I would see remarkable physical and vocal skills. He wasn't wrong.

The Tavern had a shiny topped bar that swept through the pub. The bar top was narrow and had gentle curves. It was shiny. Later in the evening the top was cleared and the drag show began. These artists, beautifully dressed in the highest of high-heeled shoes danced and sang along it. It was an astounding feat.

John knew the artists, and at the end of the show some of them joined us. They found out I was a voice teacher and they asked for help. 'Why,' they asked, 'Is it so much harder to sing wearing high heels?' I didn't know if I could help them, but over a series of sessions we helped each other. They took their shoes off and the breath went down and the voice came out. They put their shoes back on and tried to do the same. Rehearse without shoes: feel earthed. Rehearse with shoes: try and maintain as much earthiness as possible. These artists were so diligent in their determination not only to improve their voices but also to feel safer dancing on the bar when they weren't in control of their breath, when it wasn't low. They worked so hard that we didn't need many sessions.

I did the same with the gorgeous and amazing Geraldine McEwan when she was at the National. One of her scenes required her to enter screaming in full voice. In high, high heels on a steep rake – which is a slope on the stage – on a highly polished floor. Her craft was superb but the task extremely difficult.

She was worried about losing her voice. I told her the routine I had discovered at the Royal Vauxhall Tavern.

We tried it: shoes off, breath down, shoes on. She loved it and her voice, through the muscle memory of repetition, became safe and fully expressive.

As I told these stories to the cooperate women I was working with, to my amazement some of them began to perform the routine in front of me. Off came the heels. We could hear the difference after five minutes. It worked, and they began to maintain a free and authoritative voice while in heels.

This change, carried out with dedication, was one of the many examples these ambitious women taught me. With this routine, you can wear anything you want if you first find the freedom underneath, in your breath and in your body.

Every day of my life, I say to a woman, 'You are enough. Discover your full, natural enoughness before you choose to embellish yourself.' My teacher was the man who I found at the bottom of my mother's cupboard, an enlightened Shakespeare.

Sonnet 130
My mistress' eyes are nothing like the sun;
Coral is far more red than her lips' red;
If snow be white, why then her breasts are dun;
If hairs be wires, black wires grow on her head.
I have seen roses damasked, red and white,
But no such roses see I in her cheeks;
And in some perfumes is there more delight
Than in the breath that from my mistress reeks.
I love to hear her speak, yet well I know
That music hath a far more pleasing sound;
I grant I never saw a goddess go;
My mistress, when she walks, treads on the ground.
And yet, by heaven, I think my love as rare
As any she belied with false compare.

20
FACING THE INEVITABLE

Till you have heard me in my true complaint
And given me justice, justice, justice, justice!

Hear me yourself; for that which I must speak
Must either punish me, not being believed,
Or wring redress from you. Hear me, O hear me, here!

Isabella – *Measure for Measure*

Eyeball to eyeball with the women who come to me with ambition for power and leadership, I tell them: This is my contract. I will tell you what you have to face, and how to work through it.

1. You will be looked at, and seen, and everything you do will be judged.
2. You cannot make anyone like you.
3. You can't show favouritism.
4. You will be envied and betrayed.
5. You will be interrupted and your ideas will be taken and owned.
6. You will have to speak hard truths to people.
7. You will forget what to say.
8. You will have to admit that you don't know.

9 You will have to apologize.

10 You will face fear and stress on a daily basis.

Then I explain that I will teach them the strategies they need to become a leader and face the inevitable.

1 Be present, audible and clear all the time.

2 Always prepare aloud for every meeting you know will be difficult, and practise aloud the points that you think you might have to make, even though they won't come out verbatim.

3 Don't shout unless it is the absolute last resort.

4 Don't rush, it signals fear and no one can follow speed for long. You're more likely to be interrupted when you rush.

5 Don't ramble. If you prepare aloud beforehand, you will find the words you need to be concise.

6 Speak sooner rather than later. Don't hold back your knowledge or wait too long to express yourself.

7 When you're invited to a meeting they want to hear from you. Don't be a passive listener. That will result in them ignoring you or feeling that you are hiding something.

8 Make eye contact and breathe.

9 Be kind to yourself. Women seeking perfection miss important signals and have a harder time realizing how good their own work is.

10 Be fair, be generous. Being fair sometimes means having to say hard things.

11 Take yourself and your knowledge seriously.

12 There will be loss, you will lose the fun of flirting and gossip.

If I knew a short cut I would teach it

Now we have to do the work.

The three most important things I can teach women about their voices are:

1   For you to recognize when and how your presence and voice goes wrong.

2   How to reset your voice and presence.

3   How to extend them and make them more powerful and thrilling.

But first, we need to know how we feel in our body and breath when we are uncomfortable. Being uncomfortable is often associated with not feeling safe, and if we attend to how it manifests in our body, we have a chance to control it.

My mantra is, *Where am I?* We have to ask ourselves continuously: *Where's my body? Where's my breath? Where's my presence?*

Your body

Where is your body?

Stand in front of a mirror, barefoot, wearing clothes that reveal your shape.

Face the reflection.

If you blur your eyes you can often see the general outline and placement.

Now look specifically and scan your body with acceptance.

Look at your feet.

Our body, our breath, our presence requires us to be rooted through the feet onto the earth. Make sure your feet are underneath your pelvic bones. Not too close, not too far out. If they're close together, you pull yourself into First Circle. If they're outside your pelvic area, you're pushing yourself into Third Circle.

Your natural placement means that your feet are under your hips, with the weight of your body on the front of your feet and the heels still on the ground.

Now look at the knees and pelvic area.

The knees unlocked and the pelvis on top of the legs. Not pushed forward or back.

Bones hold us up and the wrong placement of your feet, knees and pelvis weakens your foundation.

Turn sideways and see if your body is stacked up, fully aligned, without distortion, through your feet, knees and pelvic area.

If it is not, the breath cannot be fully down, and weaknesses in these physical foundations are heard in your voice. The tensions move up your body and lodge in your throat, weakening the sound and range. Your options are to sound weak or to push and sound harsh. Without full connection to the floor you will sway, wiggle or fidget. Your authority is compromised.

Now look at your stomach.

Is your stomach held in? Or too flopped out? Just observe this.

Now look at your spine, upper chest and shoulders. Is your spine slumped and pulling your chest in and your shoulders round? If so, your breath is shallow or held, and your presence is pulled into First Circle.

Is your spine rigidly pulled up? If so, your shoulders will be held back, the upper chest lifted, and you are bracing yourself into Third Circle. The pulling back or up of your shoulders disempowers your voice and makes a hard, generalized sound that bounces off listeners' ears. The shoulders should hang freely. Any physical tightness in the body will end up in your shoulders, so constant monitoring of them is very effective when you feel fear or stress.

Look at your neck, head position and jaw. 'Bottleneck' is a good description of what happens to the throat and the larynx in it, when there is any unnatural tension in the body, below the neck and above it.

Is your head balanced on the top of the spine? Looking at the world? Or looking down? Or is it pushed forward, or the chin pulled up pushing the head back? The head is heavy, and if it's not balanced on top of the spine it will squash the neck and therefore the voice.

However, if the body is not aligned then the head can't be fully balanced.

Is your jaw tight, teeth clenched? The natural 'at rest' position of the jaw is to have your lips touching but the teeth unclenched. You can feel jaw tension in the back of the throat and often see the tension in the neck. Head, jaw and neck tensions inhibit the freedom of the voice – its range, its power – and mar speech muscles, making clear articulation impossible.

Now look at your face. Is it tight across the forehead, between the eyes, lips? Is it a mask that is held or has it possible movement?

Note any physical tensions you have observed.

Move away from the mirror and perform these simple adjustments.

Be barefooted and use a tennis ball. Place your foot on the ball and roll the foot from the heel to the toe over the ball. Do this for thirty seconds and then put your foot on the floor. Feel how that foot is more connected to the floor. You might also feel the breath in that side is lower and the shoulders and upper chest more released. Repeat with the other foot.

Place your feet under your hips and stand with your weight forward on the balls of your feet and imagine that you could move in any direction starting in your feet but flowing through the whole body. You are physically alert. Your feet are connecting to the earth but can respond to any internal or external energy.

Stand with your feet under your hips, feeling the weight of your body being connected through the balls of your feet – a slight shift forward onto the front of the foot will do this. Circle your pelvis round, keeping your knees and ankles flexible. Try to feel your legs supporting the pelvis, which should be balanced on top of the legs, not pushed forward or pulled back.

Concentrate on your spine. Slump and then pull up too far on the spine. Feel how the sternum responds – the slump collapses the chest, the rigid spine hardens the chest. Swing both arms around and then suspend them up to the sky. Remember to have your weight forward, knees unlocked. As the arms come down and return to the side, the spine should be more naturally placed.

Move your shoulders up and down, then around and then gently swing one arm around as if you were throwing a ball underarm. Let it return to hanging by your side. Repeat with the other arm. You will feel more energy in your hands.

Move the head from side to side. Raise the chin and see if you can identify a moment when the head is balanced on the spine, not looking down, pushing forward or pulling back. Move all your facial muscles. Bunch them up and release them. Massage the face and jaw gently. Unclench the teeth and feel that the lips can be together without jaw tension.

Now flop over forward from the waist. Keep the weight on the balls of your feet, knees unlocked, shoulders released and arms hanging loosely down.

Slowly come up without pushing the pelvis forward. Stack the spine up and allow the shoulders to find their own place.

Head should be the last placement and balanced on top of the spine.

Go to a wall and gently push against it with one foot in front of the other and no lifting in the shoulders or upper chest, the pelvis on top of the legs so you can access your full breath power, arms not over-stretched and head up, looking into the wall.

Breathe and then come away from the wall. You should feel more centred and secure in your body and the breath should be lower; you will feel it moving down.

Return to the mirror and work with the adjustments in front of it. Stand sideways and check on your pelvis, spine and position of the shoulders.

Notice any shifts?

As you study yourself, you are present with yourself.

Take that presence away from the mirror and look with it around the space you are in.

Breath

Return to the mirror. Now look at your breath moving your body. Where do you see movement? Are you taking time to fully breathe? Is your intake noisy, through your nose or mouth?

A natural inspiration of breath should not lift the shoulders, upper chest or be gasped. Your ribs should move out around the sides, and the breath should particularly open the back of the ribcage.

After the ribs have opened, there should be movement down into the abdominal area, as deep as the groin.

Place your hands – without lifting the shoulders – firstly on your ribcage and then after you've breathed in and out a few times, move them from the sides to the same position on your back. As you breathe in, the ribs should open out and then move in to support the outward breath.

Next, place a hand on the stomach just above the groin and see if you can feel an outward movement there on the inspiration, and then an inward movement as you breathe out. Return your arms to your sides and look again. Any lift in the shoulders or chest, any restriction in the ribcage and stomach, disempowers your voice.

Take time to breathe, and see if you can feel and observe that crucial moment of suspension when the breath you need is taken in and the breath muscles suspend to change direction before you breathe out. Recognizing this suspension can be hard, but it is crucial, because as soon as you do it, you can fully power your voice. This happens when your breath is under the sound, the word, the ideas and feelings. The breath is doing the equivalent of a hand strumming guitar strings. As I said above, you cannot play a guitar without that hand touching the strings and you cannot play your voice until low breath touches the vocal folds.

Move away from the mirror and make the three following adjustments to the breath. Be aware of the physical adjustments that you have already done in the body, as it and the breath are connected and meshed together.

Stand centred. Flop over to one side, bringing the arm on the outward side of the flop in an arch sideways over your head like the top half of the letter 'C', and with your other arm, pull down gently on the wrist of that arm. Breathe slowly and deeply. You should feel the stretched side move around the ribcage. After a few breaths, stand up and allow the shoulders to release. As you breathe you should feel more movement on the stretched side. This is the ribcage on that side opening. Repeat on the other side. When you come up to standing you might feel the upper chest lift and move, so place a hand on it to still it. Don't let the sternum hoist.

This is a major breath stretch and can make you dizzy and/or emotional. It opens the back of the ribcage and engages the lower breath and support.

Stand centred. Hug yourself by wrapping your arms around you without lifting the shoulders and keeping the arms touching your chest. Breathe in and out aiming to feel the back ribcage open. Still hugging, flop over forwards so that your torso is hanging from the waist, arms still touching the chest, shoulders released. Release the back of your neck as much as you can. Keep energy forward in your feet and knees unlocked. Take several full, slow and calm breaths. Feel the back open, feel the stomach release. Feel the suspension on the breath after you have taken a full breath. Feel the muscles of support under the outward breath. Still in the same position, release your arms and then slowly come up, rolling up through the spine and return to centre. You might be dizzy, but when that fades can you feel the breath deeper and the centre of your body wider? You are taking up the space you have the right to fill.

After these two exercises, go to the mirror and see if you can spot any difference in the deeper placing of the breath.

Fully empowering your breath

The work you've done on your body and breath is sufficient if you don't want full empowerment. But now I have to re-state that the power of our body, mind and heart is based in the breath. And it's a very rare occurrence for me to meet a Western woman who has maintained her natural breath.

Women have no chance of meeting their full potential without being able to take a full, natural breath. Women gasp, we hear the breath, a sign of weakness to any predator, taking short, shallow intakes of the life force of oxygen. Women sigh out their power, deflating their body through their ribcages. We hold our breath for long periods of time, sometimes to the extent of inducing panic attacks.

Deep placing of the breath

This exercise engages a deep, natural breath.

It takes time and should be done in a safe, warm place. You shouldn't expect to get up from this work and be dynamic. It is good to do it before bed and will make you sleep better.

My warning is that it can make you feel emotional because you touch your full power. So stop if it gets overwhelming.

Find a heavy book. *The Complete Works of Shakespeare* will do! You'll need a chair that is a comfortable height so that you can lie on the floor on your back and rest your calf muscles on the seat of the chair.

Have a thin cushion to rest your head on.

Place the book on the lower abdomen. This will aid you in feeling a low, full breath and the suspensions between the breath.

Slow your breath down.

Start with your arms above your head.

Breathe and allow the floor to gradually take all the weight of your arms. Some shoulder tensions are so deep that the full release of your arms might take a few weeks, so you should keep doing the full exercise every day until this happens.

After a while, bring your arms round so that they lie beside you – keep breathing all the time. If you feel the upper chest lift, put one hand on the sternum. Put your hands on the sides of your ribcage as you breathe, so that you can feel them open. Then slide them round behind your back, and see if you can feel that it's opened more. When the upper chest is still and the ribs are opening and you feel how deeply you can move the book on your abdominal area, you are taking a full, natural breath. Be aware of how long you can wait before you need breath, and how long the suspension can be before you breathe out.

Do this for twenty minutes. Then take the book off the abdomen and feel how deep the breath is. After a few minutes, roll over onto your side, get onto your hands and knees and come up slowly.

Keep breathing as you get up.

Now centre yourself and you will feel more aligned and connected with the lower breath.

Begin to work the breath to develop power for volume, vocal freedom and flexibility.

Repeat the exercises you did earlier, stretching the sides of the ribcage and the back.

Move over to face a wall. Put one foot in front of the other and place both hands on the wall, the arms bent, not with locked elbows. Make sure your knees are unlocked and that there is no lift or tension in the shoulders or upper chest. The pelvis should be on top of your legs, not with your bottom sticking out. Your spine should be up and your head looking into the wall. As you breathe, you should feel the breath settle low in your breath system. Now, fully concentrate on feeling the suspension of the breath – the moment it engages and the moment it releases. Still pushing against the wall, when you feel the breath is ready, release on a light *Sssssss*. Come away from the wall, and see if you can feel a deeper connection to the breath.

Begin to feel the intake of breath suspend as you breathe in and before you breathe out.

Feel the stretch into the back and around the sides of the ribcage, and feel the lower breath connections in the abdomen. Aim to feel the breath suspension and then release the breath on a *Sssssss*. Go as far as you can before you begin to run out of breath and can no longer make the sound without squeezing. This will coincide with restrictions in the shoulders, spine or jaw.

Swinging as though throwing a ball underarm will enhance this feeling. The push or throw starting the breath connection. Return to a push whenever you feel the breath disconnect. Try to build up the release on *Sssssss* over twenty seconds. Then doing seven repeats on *Sssssss* one after another.

Then you can begin build-up, counting. Take a breath, count *One*. Take a breath, count *One*, *Two*. Build up over fifteen counts. Keep the breath low and as slow as possible to return to a natural breath pattern. After fifteen, send the counts around the room, to put you into Second Circle. This occurs when you look at a specific point in the room, take a breath while looking at it and sending it out to that point. Really take time to get the breath *in*.

There used to be a term – *the hysterical breath*. This is a high, short breath that can be seen in the lift of the sternum. The name hysterical is rooted in the Greek word for womb. In other words, a 'woman's' breath pattern. This high breath, if pursued to its final destination, results in a panic attack, and probably the breather passing out so that the natural breath can take over and keep you alive!

This pattern and high rhythm of breath is rarely seen in men.

It is artificially manufactured when a tight corset is put on. The ribs are squashed and the only place to breathe is in the totally inefficient and underpowered upper chest. I remember years ago having the light-bulb moment as to why so many Victorian women in novels were fainting over quite minor shocks. Their ribcages couldn't cope with the need to take a bigger breath so they keeled over.

Breath does not only keep us alive, but we require different amounts to navigate a larger voice, a passionate feeling or idea, flight or fight, or emotional shock. The corset blocks the wearer from being able to take a large breath. There is such a long history of erotic excitement centred on women wearing clothes that stop them breathing or otherwise restrict them. Presumably, it's exciting to a certain kind of man because the woman is then unable to run away. The choice-less habits are quite possibly bedded into a body because they have been rewarded: the woman is going to be cared for and protected.

Whatever the choices or rewards involved, by the time I meet my female students who are around the age of eighteen to twenty-one, very few of them have retained any semblance of a naturally powerful and fluid breath system.

The full breath

To take a full breath is not only fully empowering, but centres a human being, relaxes you, calms you and clears out trauma.

Watch a dog after a bout of barking: they will turn around a bit, flop down, sigh and take a good deep breath to reset their emotional clock and eradicate the reason for the bark.

Humans should do the same so that they can clean out any unpleasantness or shock and return to being in the moment without the impediments in the breath the upset produced.

It is impossible to take a full breath if the necessary equipment is blocked. Slumping the spine, rounding the shoulders and locking the knees stops the full breath. But what most women do is hold their stomach in. This is a habit so deeply ingrained it can be very difficult to unlearn.

The complete lock or stopping of the breath

In corporate coaching I am constantly hired to empower female employees who have been undermined or more crudely bullied by a manager. I ask them to think about the bullies' presence and what happens to them when their predator enters their space. I ask them to notice what happens to their body. And they have all noticed that their breath stops. In any frightening or uncomfortable space, we try not to be noticed by not taking a full breath, locking the whole system up for several seconds at a time. A full stop of breath making you live in a temporary vacuum.

Imagine a mouse with a hawk or cat hovering nearby. It has two options for survival. The first is *flight* but not *fight*, as there is no way of winning. But, if there is no place to run to or hide, they also have the option of becoming so still that they might not be seen. The only way to achieve full stillness is to stop breathing; to *hold the breath*.

Every woman who has experienced domestic abuse, walked alone at night or entered a darkened car park . . . every woman in the savage workplace, experiences this *lock*. And sometimes the trauma of that lock stays with them for the rest of their lives.

So many women have told me: 'I stop breathing.' By stopping the breath, they are acting like the mouse. *I can't run, I can't fight – but I might not be noticed if I go still and stop breathing.*

In a mouse this reaction lasts for a few seconds, not throughout days and years. Of course, these women *are* breathing, but in such a sporadic way that their existence in the workplace is a disempowered hell that often spills over into the rest of their life. Or, it can start the other way around. I can remember that when I was a child, when my drunk father's key turned in the door, I stopped breathing.

Women have to learn to fully breathe again without locks and with flow. Empowered breath is always moving, *in, suspension, out, suspension*, like the sea. It never stops until you stop.

Interestingly, I have experienced and always teach that by maintaining an unlocked breath system in the presence of a bully you will notice that most stop bullying you. I teach: stay in Second Circle and *breathe to them, breathe to them, breathe to them.* They won't know why, but it works. All you need to do is breathe out towards them calmly and silently. You're centring yourself at the same time.

We cannot underestimate how much these simple anatomical signals inform the world about our own sense of power or lack of it.

I have had raw and painful sessions when a bully – so valuable to a company that HR is fighting off serious complaints from employees as to this person's abusive behaviour – is sent to me. Many of them have acknowledged that they know who they can intimidate, and even recognize that the signal is in the locked 'mouse breath'.

It's crucial to remember that none of this is the 'victim's' fault. At some point, not breathing has worked for them. It has been rewarded with success, that is, not being seen in a room. But if you don't refind your breath, under pressure you will verge towards panic and forget what you know you know. You'll be unable to get into a discussion or conversation, or, if you do manage to utter, it will be at the wrong moment. It will be clumsy, rushed and vocally tight.

Not breathing at all stops you being able to listen, so you will miss the wave that enables you to say what you want to say at the appropriate moment.

The sigh

The sigh is a release of breath that resets our breath system after strong emotion. Remember, anyone who has comforted a crying baby knows that you gently rock her, to soothe and calm her – and you instinctively wait and hold her after the crying has stopped. You wait for a sigh, and once that has come, you know that whatever has upset her has left her breath system. Now she will settle. If you put her back to bed before the sigh she won't go back to sleep!

Adults do this too, but most of us only recognize this after we have had a good laugh or cry; then we naturally sigh to reset our systems.

Because of all the stress and fear in women's breath systems, a lot of us sigh not only after an emotional release, but a lot of the time. The sigh is natural, but not when it is used constantly and divorced from a heightened release. Used inappropriately it constantly deflates physical and vocal power. As we excavate deeper into these habits we have to understand that they signal subliminal messages to those around us. Sighing inappropriately signals *weakness*, *giving up*, *pessimism*. A sigher bleeds energy out of the room. It can disempower a group. It can depress a group. A sigher can use the sigh consciously or unconsciously to communicate, 'I can't be bothered,' 'You are a nuisance,' 'You're so stupid,' 'Notice how hard done by I am,' or most of all, 'Poor me'. All negative and debilitating emotions.

It is often the tactic of someone who feels disempowered and can't express it in words. A silent contempt for power.

Let us return to the three stages of breath.

Breathe in

Suspension, when the breath is suspended and ready to breathe out – the feeling on a swing as it reaches its height and suspends before it moves down.

After suspension breath muscles move in to *expel* air and the voice.

A confident speaker speaks on the breath. A sigher breathes in, suspends and sighs out the power before they speak. If you do this, you must practise speaking on the breath. This can be achieved with the exercises we've already done – pushing against the wall, or imagining you're throwing a ball underarm, taking a breath as the arm moves back, and releasing a breath on the suspension of the arm. If you can, actually get a ball and throw it against a wall, catch it and throw again, and start speaking as you throw. This will get you speaking on the breath.

Rushing the breath

This is the opposite of sighing. It is speaking when you're not ready and have not taken enough breath. This breath habit leaves you tripping over words and gabbling; the most common habit in women seeking power. Heart-breaking, as most have enormous knowledge. But the rushing is not only impossible to listen to, it also signals panic, low confidence and powerlessness. This can be linked to the fear of being interrupted or of being boring. It can also be a Third Circle power play – *I'm talking now*. The slow, deep breath will start to reset your breath muscles so that you speak when you're ready, not before.

I am citing huge disempowering habits of the breath system. I rarely meet a woman without one of them, if not all in some form.

Let us put presence into the body and the breath.

Take a slow, deep breath that doesn't lift your shoulders or upper chest. You should feel the ribcage open all around – particularly the back of the cage. Make sure you feel the release of the intake as deeply into your lower abdominal muscles as you can.

When you feel the fullness of the breath and its suspension, breathe out, sensing that the power of the breath is being controlled by the muscles of the ribs and abdominal area. Go as far as you can without squeezing or tightening the sternum or spine.

Breathe out to a point outside yourself. Breathe fully into your space, all that you can see, in order to take enough breath to touch and fill that space. Your breath reaching out in Second Circle. Sending your power and authority into the world. Calm, strong, clear and sensitized to all that's around you.

Now feel what happens if you hold your breath, sigh or rush, lift the shoulders and upper chest, hold the stomach in. All these tensions of intake disempower your breath and presence.

Return to the full power position of the centred body and full deep breath.

Where is your presence?

Over the years, I've realized that you can't address your presence until your body and breath have returned to their natural alignment and power. Negative tensions in the body or breath – all that we have just discussed – desensitize and inhibit our presence.

Second Circle balance

The single most powerful thing you can do to survive, to stay engaged, to appear with authority, is to remain present in Second Circle. Any distraction can leave you open to losing your presence and your power. The first technique that enables you to do this is staying connected in your body and breath. Even if you have worked tirelessly on the placing and sculpting of your body, without presence and breath it is disconnected.

The simplest way to *feel presence* is to walk with purpose, looking out at the world around you. Not over-striding, not walking in a 'cool' way, but a direct walk, moving forward. As you do this exercise, try changing direction as cleanly as possible, and every now and then stop, and see where your body is. Immediately after stopping you are going to be more physically centred and breathing deeply. Notice if you want to pull back into First or push forward into Third, and be aware of the accompanying tensions that produces.

A more powerful way of doing this exercise is walking purposefully on rough ground.

As you do this, notice that your breath becomes deeper, and that your feet, ankles, knees and upper body respond to the uncertain terrain and will gradually return you to a more centred and aligned physical placement. And you will feel more present. Quite simply, our bodies are not designed to walk for hours on hard, flat surfaces. Paved cities contribute to a huge amount of our physical distortion – from knees to spine to shoulders to jaw, the relentless pounding of hard streets on our bodies and breath reverberates through the feet to the head.

An acquaintance lived for several years in the desert with the Bedouins. Walking on sand and rocks, sharp and jagged surfaces. One day, he took three Bedouin youths into their first paved city. In under an hour of walking on flat, hard surfaces, they were in agony throughout their bodies. We are all in agony but have been desensitized to the trauma of the street poundings on and in our body and presence.

A few years after I heard this story, I was working with a group of corporate leaders who were also Bedouin. I recounted this tale to them and they laughed at me, saying 'Of course!' They had all experienced the same thing in their own cities, and many of them added that they still regularly went out to walk in the desert, to refind their bodies and themselves.

Work and preparation for Third Circle speakers

1   Make real eye contact – don't look beyond or above heads. Stand with feet underneath your hips, with the weight on the balls of your feet. Knees unlocked. Avoid standing with feet too far apart.

2   The pelvic area should balance on top of your legs, not thrust forward. Place a hand just above your groin and encourage movement in your stomach as you breathe.

4   Circle the arms, with flow and ease, and as they come to a standstill don't brace or place them.

5   Place a hand on your sternum and then let it drop. You will feel the back of the ribcage relax. The upper chest should soften.

6   Release your jaw. Feel the lips touching but the teeth unclenched underneath.

7   Without pushing your chin forward, gently stroke the front of your neck and feel it relax.

8   Hand flat on your sternum. Breathe in silently through the nose and then the mouth, without the upper chest or shoulders lifting. Now the other hand on your stomach and try to feel gentle movement there. Take time.

9   Your spine should be held up but not rigidly. There should be a softening throughout your body. Hug yourself and flop over from your waist. Breathe, aiming to feel the back of your ribcage

open and movement down to your abdominal area. As you
come up, breathe slowly in and out, let your arms go and feel
the ribcage move more freely.

10 Feel the readiness to speak on the inward breath by swinging
your arm back as you breathe in, as though you were about
to throw a ball underarm. Too much energy in the swing will
force the air in, and there will be a tendency to release
before the body feels the required suspension for full and
unforced vocal power. Speak as you feel the connection to
the breath.

11 Breathe *to* a person or group, not beyond them.

Work – Low tension – First Circle speakers

1 Make real eye contact. Don't look halfway towards people.
Don't look down, glaze your eyes or avoid eye contact.

2 Stand with your feet underneath your hips, weight on the balls
of your feet, knees unlocked. Feet not too close together.

3 Lift up through your spine. There will be a tendency to slump
your spine. Stretch up to the Goddesses and as your arms
come down keep the spine up.

4 Windmill your arms around gently to release shoulders, and as
they come down, don't pull the shoulders in or round them.
Keep the upper chest open.

5 Place your hand on your upper chest and if you feel that it's
depressed, pulling you down, lift it up.

6 Release the jaw and make sure that as you do, you lift the
upper cheek muscles – think of a smile – to engage more
energy in your face.

7 Lift your head up until you feel it balanced on top of your spine.
Not tilted or tucked down.

8 Stretch your ribs and lower breath by hugging yourself and
flopping over. Really take time to fully breathe.

9 Push against a wall to feel the power in your lower breath and ribs opening. When you feel the breath low, still pushing, release on a voiced *Zzzzzz* and try to sustain this sound steadily. Repeat at least five times and build up muscle in your breath system. When you come away from the push on the wall, the breath around the centre of the body will feel stronger.

10 Breathe *to* people and groups, not halfway to them.

21
WHERE IS YOUR VOICE?

Your natural, free voice

As we breathe in, we gather energy. As we breathe out, we send our energy into the world. This includes our voice and our words. The power of the voice should be fully given out, not blocked or hidden by holding sound in. The natural voice flows out without impediments. The natural voice moves up and out of us in an arc, and when the throat is open and the voice is released you don't feel tension in your throat. The voice should not be pushed down into the chest, which muffles and inhibits it. Not forced out with tension in the throat: this is not power. Not on half-power that sounds fuzzy and is the start of a whisper. Not being pulled back into the mouth or jammed behind the jaw. This doesn't only stop audibility, but masks what we say with tensions. This tension filters the voice so that the words cannot be fully heard but are interpreted through the vocal sieve. An unfree voice is hard to listen to and because it cannot move freely, generalizes meaning and flattens out ideas and feelings.

A free voice is not felt in you but lives in the space outside you. A great soprano once told me, 'I imagine that I don't have a throat. I feel the energy of my breath move up through my body so that my voice lives outside me.' In this way, the voice and words leave you and exist in space. The Ancient Greeks believed that when you speak in this way, words create something concrete and you have to stand by what you say, which has historically been a problem for women, because when we do this, we commit, and the words can't be called back. Most of us have been punished for committing to what we say.

Even when women have the spirit and strength to speak out, to commit, the historic habits can appear: a quiet, hard-to-hear voice without proper physical freedom and breath power, a harsh, pushed, angry sound. A whine. Vocal tones that don't match the content, so even if the voice is loud and words clearly spoken, the meaning is unclear.

Women who are leaders still have problems saying exactly what they *feel* if they have trained themselves to be super-rational in defiance of the male idea that women are too emotional. They have less exposure to addressing elders, and when they do, it can overwhelm them so that they lose their authentic voice, falling back on non-threatening behaviour.

Women bite their tongue! They don't say something important, or do say it when it's not appropriate.

We still rely too much on sympathetic listeners. Our voices still swing between the two worlds of First and Third Circle, and this is heard in our voice, even if we have worked on our body and breath.

From de-voicing to pushing.

From little girl voice, to rushing.

Being too precise or too casual.

Overstressed or under-stressed.

From boring to over vocal exaggeration.

All these issues can be addressed and balanced when we refind our natural and freely produced and released voice.

We can start the work now.

Warming up your voice

Throughout these exercises keep the body centred and the breath low and connected to the sound.

Massage your face and gently smile and open your jaw with your smile in place. This opens the throat.

Bunch up your facial muscles and allow them to release. Let the muscles find the position they want to be in. The natural position is the lips touching but without the teeth being clenched.

The smile opens the throat and this effect can be felt even when you think of a smile.

A free voice should not be felt in the throat. The space in the throat should be open without the slightest friction. If you can hear any noise as you breathe in through the mouth, then the throat is not fully open.

Tension in the throat traps the voice and gives it a stuck tone or quality. Even the smallest grip holds your voice. A very tight throat will tire, or at worst, damage the voice. If you feel the neck and the voice tightening at any point, think of a yawn. The throat will open.

The voice leaves us on an arc. Up and out.

Stand and breathe.

Find a point above your eye line and breathe to it.

Take the full breath and hum gently onto the lips. Aim to feel a buzz there. This is an indication that the voice is moving forward. There should be no tension in the throat.

Repeat the hum and take it into an *OOO* placing the lips forward and aiming for a point above your eye line.

Repeat until you feel the voice freely moving forward.

Now add an *AHH*.

Breathe and release *OOO* into *AHH*.

Several releases on this will begin to strengthen and open your voice.

Embodying this could include your arm and hand indicating the arc of your voice coming up through your head and out to the point above your eye line.

Your voice will be warmed up with these exercises.

Warm up your resonators

The vibration of the vocal folds creates the sounds, but without the body and the resonators within it, the human voice would sound like a bumblebee wrapped in a handkerchief.

Its richness, tone and amplification happens in physical cavities throughout the body – resonators; like the box of a guitar.

The main resonators of the human voice are chest, throat, face, nose and head.

The size of each resonator and the state of muscles around them affects the quality and richness of the voice.

With breath, hum into your head, aiming to feel a buzz there. Hum into the nose – feel the buzz there.

Hum into the mouth and onto the lips.

All the time, feel the arc and don't run out of breath – feel the sound has breath underneath it.

Warm up the chest resonator by humming into the upper chest, but avoid sitting on the voice by pushing down on the larynx and constricting the throat. The image of *up and out* releases this tension.

This sitting on the voice by pushing down on the larynx is the most common habit in women seeking vocal authority. This creates a vocal strain and a tone that is trapped. It can hurt the voice and even damage it.

You can open and deepen your voice without pushing down on it by doing the exercise above and sending the voice out on an arc.

This takes more breath but is a strengthening exercise that enriches your tone.

Now try an *OO* into an *AH,* feeling the sound move through all of your resonators.

If you are pushing the voice down into the throat, or pulling it back into the mouth, or dropping off the energy, go to a wall, and push to connect the breath and then vocalize, still pushing *OO* into *AH.* Come away from the wall and play by sending these sounds to different points in the room.

Warming up your range

Change of pitch requires a free and flexible voice and throat. The voice should move easily through various notes, expressing passion, thought and feeling. A limited range will bore your audience. Pitch changes happen through the lengthening and thickening of the vocal folds, but we can warm up and stretch these folds with some simple exercises.

I remind you to remember the work we have just done in the body, presence, breath and resonators. Stretch the range by humming or hah-ing down, and then up, through your vocal range. Thinking *up and out*, particularly on the lower notes.

Come down in this way, staying on breath and centred without the head moving up and down. And then move up through your range.

Now, without moving the head, aiming at some point across the space, count down through all your range and then count up through all your range. Do this at least four times, making sure that breath is always under there. Take the sound *Ma-Ma-Ma* and move all through your range, in a playful way.

Now you should feel a stronger and more flexible voice.

Speech

Speech requires an even more complex activity. When we speak, we mould the energy of the voice into words through the lips, tongue, soft palate and teeth. If the voice is not placed forward in the mouth and released, many of the speech muscles cannot feel the energy, and therefore cannot perform effectively. This is why speech work is considered the last activity of the communication chain.

Clarity is reliant on clear and muscular articulation.

Speech muscles require constant work and preparation: the clear manufacturing of words is a complex dance of muscles in the mouth with the tongue and lips, jaw and soft palate.

For success you need to open your mouth and pronounce every syllable. We habitually forget to say the ends of words and all the syllables in multi-syllabic words. This habit is heard in men as well as women, but I have often seen that this lack of clarity is more ignored when men do it.

Lack of speech clarity also contributes to women rushing. Although the depth and calmness of breath is critical to pace, speech clarity is also important.

To put it simply, you can speak and be clear as long as you can articulate all the consonants of the word.

If you don't articulate, then you cannot be understood.

The relief when we hear every word! This signals a clarity of mind and intent. If I miss words when you speak I will miss whole sections of what you say and eventually give up trying. If the rest of the apparatus is working, then it's easy to improve clarity.

As you work the speech muscles your articulation improves. You will need to give the same weight to every syllable of every word and to be diligent about finishing words, not slipping over them.

Speech muscles get fit quickly when worked, and you might go through a phase of feeling that the striving for clarity is too much. But you will work through that and soon notice the benefits of people staying to listen to you, and not asking again and again for you to repeat what you say.

If you listen carefully to a woman rushing, you will hear that consonants and syllables are missed or skidded over. A quick exercise to help the rushing is to concentrate on complete speech definition. In this way you can speak rapidly and be clear – but remember, this fast speaking can only be done occasionally as the listener cannot live with *rush* for long. Fast delivery gives texture, and if it matches the content and is used sparingly, can be very effective.

Clarity of speech helps you to stay in the moment and have time to think. This is the most sought-after impact any professional speaker aims for: to be in the moment, and mean what you say as you say it. Mind, heart and the muscle of the word marry together to produce direct and authentic communication. Communication that is exact and not random. Real impact. You cannot be misunderstood.

When you need to say something directly, every word matters, and as long as your voice releases freely out of you in Second Circle, then you will be heard, even if the listeners do not want to hear. They will be compelled to listen.

This is the moment when, if you can put the whole packet of body, breath, voice and now speech together, with full presence, you can deliver your voice and be a professional speaker.

Stand or sit with presence and a low breath. Hum to feel the forward position of the voice and imagine the arc sending sound across space. Use an *OO* to get the voice forward so that its energy can mould words through the speech muscles.

On the breath, build up a series of Ms – *ma-ma-ma-ma* – Ps – *pa-pa-pa-pa* – jaw released, and the lips touching each other with strength and then a quick neat release.

Repeat Ws – *wa-wa-wa* – which brings your lips forward.

Now a series of Ds – *da-da-da-da-da* – and Ts – *ta-ta-ta-ta-ta*. Feel the strength of the tongue on the ridge below your top teeth.

Now the Ns. Now Ls. *Na-na-na-na-na* – *la-la-la-la-la*.

Now work the back of the tongue and soft palate by pushing the tip of the tongue up to the bottom of the mouth on the gums of the lower front teeth.

Repeat K, G, NG. *Ka-Ka-Ka-Ka* – *Ga-Ga-Ga-Ga* – *Nga-Nga-Nga-Nga*. Build up speed.

This series of exercises can be done quickly in a couple of minutes and will rapidly improve your diction.

Do these exercises regularly and speech will become clear and effortless.

Even if you do these adjustments and exercises for ten minutes a day, your voice will improve, strengthen and have noticeable impact. Even better, take a poem or text, and read it out aloud, thinking of all that we have done above.

The other crucial check is whether all the words you are saying really matter, or are you speaking a lot of random words. There is no need to be clear with words that are fillers or expressions that are lubricating your thoughts or are there to give you time to think. If you want to be taken seriously as a powerful communicator then you have to accept that you need to be disciplined and economic with words. Informal and casual conversations, chit-chat or gossip is not required to be exact or formed, but important communication is.

A pause to think is powerful as long as you don't stop breathing and do hold the idea you are seeking. If you fill it with random phrases, you are diluting your message. This exactness has to be practised, and your language clarity improves quickly if you dare to wait and find the word you really need.

A sign of real authority is a pause filled with intent. This is rarely seen in women, but the ones who do it are perceived as confident and powerful.

To reiterate my point above, a very common female habit is rushing and gabbling.

This is often an attempt to show how much you know, to get it over with, or to avoid interruption. It doesn't work. Our brains can't keep up, and probably your brain is ahead of the words so you are precariously flying along but could stumble at any time. The audience feels this. The compassionate ones worry about you, the less kind ones wait for you to stumble.

Women work harder at these techniques than men do. Maybe because they receive negative feedback more than men. This work ethic can lead to women making some well-meaning mistakes.

They want their presentations to be perfect.

Instead of making notes or bullet points, they write out the whole presentation word-for-word, which is not helpful. The written word is different from the spoken word, and sounds less available, too formal, unless it is skilfully worked.

Then they learn it by heart, which is generally catastrophic.

Prepare your presentation or meeting out loud with clear points in your journey. Let it be free enough for you to improvise, as long as your journey is exact. (If you have to have the whole speech written – for legal reasons, for example – know it well and practise it aloud.) But have your speech with you. If you need to look at it, look at it, get your eyes off the page, look at the audience and carry on.

If you are speaking in any formal setting you are being looked at and everything you do is noticed. You cannot hide, and it looks ridiculous if you behave as if you think you are invisible. Surreptitiousness looks duplicitous.

When you make a mistake, carry on if it's small, but if it is big then you may need to acknowledge it. Powerful men do this as well.

The huge advantage of coming into a space fully present and making eye contact with the audience is that you break the wall between you and them. This allows you to reach out to them, and that could mean coming off your written text and speaking to them. This humanizes you, the space and the audience.

This interaction, the dialogue with the audience, is one of the greatest signs of leadership and balanced power; it's Second Circle.

I've made you think about all the components of your voice, which can be very annoying! But I never want you to think about your voice when the full flow of communication is happening. As you work regularly, your free voice will become organic and be there for you all the time.

When this happens the sound of a voice marries with sense and the full impact of your meaning enters the listener.

If the sound of the voice is in a counterpoint to the meaning, then it confuses. The voice sounds *this* way but the meaning is moving *that* way. For instance, sarcasm is formed with this split and conflict between voice and language. The root of the word sarcasm is from the Greek and means 'the tearing of flesh'. When someone is being sarcastic, the *words* might seem kind, but the *tone* belies that.

Direct and honest communication has to be the voice and language working together.

When I teach leadership and formal communication, this honest directness is ethically non-negotiable if a leader is to use their power responsibly.

You have to understand that no vocal games or confusion should appear in your communication.

For those without power it is understandable that sound and sense might not match. It is a way of saying something contentious without being imprisoned – satire and the political impact behind nursery rhymes are examples of this.

It seems logical that women – who have not historically had power – have sourced all sorts of vocal habits to say what they need to say without being direct. As women gain full power they must relinquish these habits and games.

You might have to sacrifice some of the fun voices and forms of communication you have used.

22
MASKS OF SURVIVAL

The little girl, the flirt, the sweet voice, the laughing voice, the conceding voice, the flattering voice.

These habits come from the need to be liked and found attractive. The need to not threaten men. The need to not show higher intelligence. To not be too serious, but to demonstrate that we have a sense of humour even when the joke is on us. Masks of survival for those who have had no power for thousands of years.

I don't blame any woman for adopting any of the above, but you have to realize that when you're in power, there is a price to be paid if you do.

As I've said, I started teaching in 1975 when the feminist movement was gathering momentum. Legislation had given women legal rights. The debate about equality was passionate, current and vigorous.

My mother's generation tended to pitch their voices *up*. To sound more 'feminine'. More acceptable to the male ear. My mother even had friends who would change their vocal pitch upwards when a man entered the room or when they were on the telephone to a man.

Overnight, feminist women were pushing *down* on their voices – in order to imitate men's power. They were not finding their own voices; another mask on their natural voice. Some of my first teaching assignments were with women who asked me to help them safely lower their voices.

The higher voice is also a mask. It's only a part of your full voice. One very powerful woman who did lower her voice from one that was too high was Margaret Thatcher in the late seventies. But she lowered it too much, and it sounded unnatural, and she frequently became husky because of this misuse.

The game voices – the little girl, the flirt, the sweet, the laughing – are all masking a woman's full powerful and authentic voice. They filter only a part of who we are to the world. These voices are choices, maybe not made in a fully conscious way. But they have been consistently rewarded by men and sometimes other women.

It was hard for my mother's generation not to use masks. It is hard today, but I feel strongly that if we choose these masks these days, we have to accept a responsibility for them.

In some ways, these disguises, although they do make some of our personal and professional journey easier, reduce us, and could eventually destroy us. There is a price to pay.

It is hard to be in the presence of unsympathetic men who do not want you as an equal. They want you to flirt, to talk about them – not about anything to do with you – to laugh at their bad if not salacious jokes, agree with them, not prove them wrong, enjoy their demeaning of you. But, the overwhelming experience that many women have shared with me about their work is that masks didn't ultimately get them where they wanted to be. It is a survival tool, but if you choose a mask for life, one that you find harder and harder to take off, it will destroy your power and any important ideas you might want to utter.

And it will exhaust you.

The mask of the smile

There is a real smile, or one that is fixed, unauthentic. Not a smile of joy or kindness, but one that signals 'Like me,' 'Be nice to me,' 'I'm a nice person.'

If you are smiling when it is not appropriate to smile, it confuses. The fixed smile is tense and locked: a real smile is fluid. A fixed smile locks the voice, generally creating a thinner tone.

I was coaching a top manager in a multinational company. Her critics – her team, her peers – called her hypocritical. When she instructed or critiqued, whatever was said, however negative the content, it was delivered with a smile. Her communication was through a mask. Her leadership was challenged because they perceived her as dishonest.

When I pointed this out she immediately understood how the smile had been useful on her way up, but that it was not applicable now that she was a leader. Some weeks working with me on facial release and consciousness around the smile managed to change her whole presence, and contributed to her ability to sound as she meant to sound. Her voice matching her words.

In some cultures, the mask-smile is deeply bedded into women's faces.

Recently I worked with a group of Japanese women who were corporate highflyers. They recognized that their fixed smiles were weakening their ability to progress. They had noticed that Western women did not have the same pressure to smile all the time. It was their request to me to help them have a clear, neutral face. Of course, their promotion opportunities were more complex, but they have reported back to me that they are taken more seriously by their male Japanese counterparts when they don't smile *all the time*.

Taking yourself seriously

There isn't a group I work with, either in theatre or the corporate world, where at least one woman doesn't do a version of the following:

An actress does a really powerful piece of work. As soon as she finishes, instead of staying with the power of the work she will put a silly face on, roll her eyes, wiggle, and in a girly voice, mock herself and her work. By doing this, she denies that she has power and laughs at, even mocks, her own good work. My comment is always, 'If you don't take your work seriously why should you expect others to?'

I know why we do this. I have been in meetings with directors and writers who didn't want to work with women who have unashamed power. They would rather be in a room with a 'silly' masked woman. They want them to deliver a role with power but be silly around them when not acting.

In the corporate world, I have coached hundreds of women who have found themselves at meetings networking, or in communication with colleagues, saying something relevant, insightful and important, but then putting on the silly mask or voice or both to demean themselves after their impressive performance!

We can stop doing this when we work on staying still and not twitching our faces, eyes or bodies. Not going into a girlie voice.

Be proud of your intelligence. Own your own power.

Flirting

Flirting can be fun but it can also be a mask blurring what should be a clear moment. This is the flirting problem I work with: you give an important note or comment about someone's work – it could be a positive remark or something that has to be worked on. Instead of listening and replying with a comment that is connected to the remark, some women – more than men – flirt! This is infuriating if you are trying to get work done. It is time-consuming and means you have to clear the moment and reset in order to go on.

Recently, I gave a constructive note to an actress. A practical note about the actual meaning of a word that she was not playing accurately. An objective note that was not contestable. She smiled, wriggled, batted her eyelids, adopted the little girl voice and said, 'Oh you're so mean.'

'No,' I said, 'I'm not. I'm giving you a note to improve your work.'

She was taken aback. All her attitudes dropped off her and she said, 'So – it doesn't work with you?'

'What doesn't work?' I asked.

'Flirting.' She laughed, and went back and did the note.

Of course the leader who is being flirted with also has a responsibility here. Not to encourage it, not to respond to it, so that it doesn't blur the work and create a sense of favouritism in a group. This is easy to do, as long as the person in control recognizes that it's their power that's being flattered, not them.

The falling line

The falling line is when you start strongly but then fall off the thought. The voice drops away. This signals a lack of directness and that the speaker is uncertain about what they're saying, which is more often than not, not true. It's another habit that's found in women much more than in men. This is a mask, hiding your intelligence and focus, and it comes from a history of being unsure that your ideas have worth.

It is also the rhythm of a lullaby: it is soothing and appeasing, but it's also in danger of sending your audience to sleep. This subconscious attempt to soothe can often backfire and sound condescending.

Take more breath to keep the voice forward, make sure that you articulate the end of every word and mean each word as you say it.

If you speak pushing against a wall, you can feel the body retreat as you fall off. This retreat looks and sounds weak and unsure when you are addressing an audience. Your intelligence is questioned or you are presumed bored – or worse, it may look as if you find the audience boring. It signals, 'It is so tedious to speak.'

Another form of falling voice happens when each word is pulled back. Unlike the falling line that happens over a thought, this pull back can be on each word. The first part of the word comes out of your mouth and you swallow the second part. It's mumbling, and sounds as though you don't care. But as soon as you realize you have to breathe and articulate to the end of every word, the habit goes.

De-voicing

De-voicing is a form of whispering. You are taking the full power out of your voice and working on half the vocal power you have. Women have used this mask for centuries. It is a First Circle half-voice that coats words with a soft quality, enabling the ability to express dangerous thoughts with a 'sweet tone'. It very often works, and is useful when you don't have power. But it can also be perceived as passive-aggressive.

The other more tangible problem is that you are inaudible if the space has more than a couple of people in it.

One of the main reasons why female de-voicers come to me for coaching is because they know no one listens to them in meetings. An audience can't hear a half-voice even in quite a small space, and even if you have a microphone on. To address this, and re-motor your full voice, you need to get your full breath and voice forward. Place your voice with an *OO* and *AH* and then intone *MA-MAY-ME*. Go straight into speaking from the intoning – you will rediscover your full voice.

Rushing

We've talked about this issue above, but it's important to reiterate.

Rushing is another mask. One that is put on because of:

- A fear that we will be interrupted.
- To show how much we know. We want to cram all our knowledge into the time we have to speak.
- Believing that rushing will stop the audience being bored – actually the reverse is true. The more we rush, the quicker people switch off.
- 'I rush because I want to get it over with!' – I've heard this so many times. But the last thing an audience wants is a signal that you don't want to be there in front of them.
- Rushing can also be a sign of high intelligence. A case of the head going ahead of your mouth. Your organs of articulation can't keep up nor can your brain imagine the words quickly enough.

To the listener, rushing says 'I have no right to be speaking.'

The deliberately held voice

Women are very aware, particularly when they are in leadership roles, that men can think that they are overemotional. Consequently, women try to combat those expectations by flattening their voices, making it too measured, too dull. One of the most thrilling and successful qualities in impactful communication is passion – so by going flat or over-measured, by not changing pace, women are depriving themselves of a most exciting and human quality in communication. I recently worked with a senior manager who had flattened her voice because she was frightened of being thought of as 'emotional', and was very upset that she'd had feedback from her team that she sounded boring. She is the treasurer in a major bank. She recognized that the hardest criticism of women's voices, particularly as they get passionate about a thought or feeling, is that they get shrill, they shriek, that the voice goes up and never comes down.

I meet this every day of my life in my work with women and their voices. An extreme example: I was recently sitting in a theatre while a young and presumably untrained actress was trying to give a powerful, emotional performance. Her voice became so shrill that five people in front of me put their fingers in their ears, the sound was so aurally disturbing. And that is what a shrill voice does to the audience. Harsh but true: you cannot complain that people are not listening if your voice hurts their ear drums. The anatomy of the piercing, harsh, shrill voice is simple. There is no breath under the sound, the emotion pushes the larynx up, and the tension in the shoulders and neck means it can't come down again.

This was the treasurer's greatest fear. I said to her, 'But you have a beautiful, free voice that is well supported with breath – let's try letting it go. Just take a breath, and let it go. You just have to trust it now. It won't go up and not come down.' She tried it, and it worked, and she's enjoying her voice again.

The jaw and mouth

When I was researching the cover for my first book *The Right to Speak* in 1991, I was looking for paintings that showed people with their mouths open. Obviously, if you don't open your mouth, sound can't come out. The right to speak is dependent on a free jaw and the mouth opening to let sound out. I couldn't find any pictures, so I approached an art historian and she looked for me, but quickly came back with this observation: 'Only the insane and prostitutes are painted with their mouths open.'

Nice girls keep their mouths shut.

Eye contact – The mask of pretending to look

Real Second Circle eye contact is powerful, and if returned, enables people to see each other's humanity and recognize each other's authority. A leader making eye contact with us makes us feel seen, known and that we matter.

If you can make full eye contact with a group or an audience, everyone feels calmer and more secure.

Women find clear, unmasked eye contact harder than men. For many women, it's been dangerous to seem this bold and questioning.

So they pretend to look, they look above you or at the floor, or don't look at all. Or, they do look and then glance away, covering the direct strong contact they have made by retreating into First Circle, belying their focus and strength. It can sometimes take my female students months to dare to look at the tall, masculine men in their group that they perceive to be powerful.

You now have all the tools to understand how to deliver your presence and voice effectively.

If you can stay present in your body, powered by the breath with the full voice leaving you, you have reached a place of full potential: physical, breath and vocal authority.

Your voice will be able to carry in all spaces. The breath dictates power, and as you take a breath that matches your Second Circle connection, you will fill the space and have impact without expecting people to struggle to hear you. As you take the breath and speak on your full voice, you will slow down and show authority, and give yourself time to think.

The free voice will move with your ideas and will have variety and sound interesting.

When you are centred on breath and your voice is open, you will not sound aggressive unless you mean to, weak unless that is your choice, your voice will not shoot up high and not come down or sound flat and dull.

Your voice is now strong, audible and clear. You have achieved *delivery* – the first stage of becoming a professional speaker.

23
FORM AND CONTENT

After delivery, we have to work on the structure (form) and content (ideas and feelings) of what we say.

As you will remember, in Ancient Greece, delivery was the first achievement that those young men learned when being taught rhetoric.

And also remember, the basic principal of rhetoric is to move people with ideas and passion.

There can be no movement in the brain until we are curious and present enough to ask a question. So we have to be in Second Circle to do this work.

Structure

Structure takes the listener on a journey. It allows the speaker to build a story or argument from the opening of a debate to exploring, and then seeking a resolve or conclusion: Open. Explore. Conclude.

This structure is at the heart of debate and is the most basic form of storytelling. It moves the ideas, stories and the speaker forward. They change as they speak, and aim to also change the listener. The movement is about progressing the speaker's and listener's heart and mind.

Structure contains, and prevents, rambling and useless repetition.

Do all the next preparation work by speaking out aloud. Even if you are writing notes or bullet points, speak as you write. This puts the words out into your mouth and helps them to engage your mind and heart. It also makes you choose the words you use and can relate to.

1   What do you need to explain? What is the question you are exploring?

2 How can you introduce that need?

3 Where do you need to go to conclude your idea or story?

Start practising where you should begin. The first thought. What ideas have to be addressed after the first thought? And then, where must your journey go in order to find a conclusion?

Form should take you, the argument and story forward. If ideas are repeated, or you move off the thrust of the journey without a real reason or choice, you could be described as a rambler. A diversion from the main road of argument has to be of value. To re-enforce a story or idea, not be a disconnected thought.

Form is a construction of ideas seeking an outcome: Beginning. Middle. End.

When you practise this basic form, of course you can break and re-order for effect. Good storytelling might begin at the end and work its way back in time.

Rhetoric also includes invention and discovery; it encourages this as you speak. The aim is to be present. Not being stuffy or prescriptive but alive, relevant and able to thrill the audience. Every question should be real, and the answer should balance the question.

The young men who study rhetoric in the powerhouses of their all-male schools learn it through *doing*. If you speak well-constructed stories, arguments and ideas out loud you will automatically learn form and feel it. Effortlessly.

What you know must be explained and practised aloud. This is a crucial step as it will lead to being a powerful presenter. You can take challenges or questions as they appear and be able to survive powerful differences of opinion with less panic or hesitation. Prepare *aloud* the answers to the questions that you dread.

Some women are so often predisposed by their upbringing to be ramblers and rushers. They feel that they have to show all they know, so they over-inform and give irrelevant information.

Women who withhold information and don't explain well are often First Circle, and the Third Circle women tend to talk too much. These speakers are in great danger of frustrating and annoying an audience.

To be effective, you must land your first moment with clarity, audibility and a relevant idea, using succinct language. Open the debate.

Structure is shape, journey and drive. Within the shape is the content. Ask yourself:

- Why do I need to speak?
- What knowledge do I have?
- Am I an expert on something?
- What do I care about in this subject?
- What is my opinion?
- What is essential that I know?
- What do I know that they don't know?

These questions will ignite content.

Content

I strongly advise you to only use your own way of speaking and language *at first*. To use words or expressions that are not usual for you can sound false initially, and just as bad, stuffy. But, if you are to communicate widely, you will soon need to extend your language and structuring skills.

You must be clearly aware of your audience. Find words and forms that suit and excite you. You have to be keen to ignite yourself in order to ignite an audience.

To sum up, there are three devices in rhetoric that can help focus your mind as you develop content. These are called the 'three modes of expression' (Aristotle). They are:

Logos – Order, reason, judgement.

This is data, facts, the law, the concrete manifestation of thought. If you are only reasonable, only speak data and facts, we are informed but bored and are not able to care about or feel the relevance of all this reason.

So we also need Pathos.

Pathos – Emotion, empathy, sympathy, feeling.

Pathos is found in the language of imagery and metaphor. In stories that ask us to feel for someone else.

It's what moves us in poems, song lyrics and plays.

But to give credibility to the stories we tell and the presentations we give, we also need *Ethos* – Moral code. Ethics. Right from wrong. Fairness. Human decency. Justice.

Ethos is the part of the content that guides our morality.

Highly successful women often know their material better than all the men around them. Many do not have the self-esteem to cut down on their factual knowledge. They have structure and data but are losing their audience. This is a clear example of Logos.

To these women, I talk about humanizing material, which loosely means telling stories to illustrate your data, but is also to encourage you to reveal your heart and morals.

I ask them to be alert to stories that pop into their heads, things they have read or remembered from personal experience, and to jot them down in a notebook.

They quickly gather a reservoir of stories and experiences that begin to fit together with their data.

Logos and Pathos begin to marry.

And then, Ethos must join them, with universal stories that teach morality.

Tell a story about someone else's behaviour, good or bad, then comment with feeling and reason, and you have mingled the three modes of persuasion.

Practise

Four rehearsal tasks.

All these tasks must be done with the full craft of Delivery:

- Presence – eye contact out into the world
- Centred and aligned body
- Low breath with its full connection to the voice
- Clear articulation

Most actors know that you have to walk into any space that requires you to be noticed and listened to with eye contact and breath.

A nervous or too casual entrance worries an audience: the first one puts them on edge, the second one signals you don't care.

You can recover the audience but it takes work, and might mean that they don't hear the first critical thoughts opening your argument.

The audience wants to feel safe with you.

So practise.

1 Silently prepare a story or piece of information you need to share.

   Stand and breathe and look around with presence as you practise *aloud* how you might tell the story.

   Don't be frightened of failing or of having to re-start.

   Struggle and find words and phrases to use.

   The advantage of speaking aloud is that you soon self-edit and within ten minutes of practising a two-minute story, you will hone and focus it more efficiently than when you write. It is a struggle to begin with but eventually spoken preparation is faster than written preparation.

   Don't rush.

   Breathe.

   Dare to wait for words and ideas in silence rather than putting in fillers: 'like', 'sort of', 'you know'.

2 Practise, in this way, the opening of the story. Practise the conclusion. Practise introducing yourself with a brief description of what you do.

3 Practise aloud the most important and perhaps the first thing you have to say in a meeting. This practise might not be exactly how you will say it, but you are preparing your mind and your words.

4 Practise difficult things you might have to say to someone aloud.

   Again, this might not be how you ultimately say it, but this drawing down of words from your brain and guiding them into your mouth will ease the pressure of an anticipated difficult conversation.

In the same way, you should practise words or phrases that you might know you should use but never do.

'Please don't interrupt me.'

'May I finish.'

'I don't think what you said is right.'

This practise is for when you know you are speaking to someone who intimidates you.

Professional conversations are formal – particularly if you have power over someone or you feel they have power over you – and should have a formal structure. This is critical if the conversations are not in public. They need boundaries around them and full presence.

You should not have to receive a negative comment casually in the corridor, and you should not be giving comments in this way. Both of you should be fully present, and ensure that consent is given for an important exchange.

You have now got the craft and the beginnings of structure and language to face and change some of the habits that weaken you when you communicate. You are equipped, and can work on the common mistakes women make in their presence, body and voice.

Where are we now?

We can claim our place at the table of power, not as handmaidens or imposters, but there in our full Second Circle presence.

We can willingly work to stay present, and to find our natural voice. We can understand what has been taken from us, and repair wounds.

We will not save the planet if women do not find their full, public voice and speak truth to power. But to lead is to risk your soul. It must be done with grace as well as strength.

EPILOGUE

Over the months of writing about The Woman's Voice, I have returned again and again to Nanna.

Her voice, her distain for the privileged classes, her eye rolls at academic knowledge being recognized as more important than common sense, and her deep contempt for the British Empire.

When I attended The Last Night of the Proms at the Royal Albert Hall, she loathed the thought of me singing *Land of Hope and Glory*.

'All that nonsense' was all she said, but there was low-level growling at the sentimentality of the British upper classes' sense of their own specialness. She had been fearless in World War II when the Germans dropped their bombs on working-class houses like hers, and growled a *fuck you* to the bombers: and here is the clue to her rage. She had lived through World War I and witnessed the carnage of a useless war. The doomed working-class men, sacrificed for nothing. The stories from Jimmy, my grandfather, who always blamed the officers for his friends' deaths.

This was in direct opposition to Mother's love of the British Empire. By the time her war came, she uncomplicatedly supported an Empire that stood its ground against the evil of fascism.

I mistook Nanna. Now I realize that she could see the good in any civilization. This seamstress could seamlessly talk to anyone, on the same level. She was curious about everyone, and wanted to understand their stories, where they had come from and where they were going. She wasn't against the good in anything, but in a way I now realize was so ahead of her time, she was against systems that oppress others and build empires. Male systems that saw the world their way, and no other. I remember an exchange we had, when she reminded me that Shakespeare came from a time when the English had no Empire, and that because of that, she could accept him. She held a fierce compassion for anyone she saw suffer, and I can see and hear her again in my female students now, who are unbound and unbowing to privilege and male power. But, unlike Nanna, they can speak with their public voices.

One of Nanna's favourite sayings was, *You can lead a horse to water, but you can't make him drink.* It was never spoken as a cliché but as a profound truth. When aimed at me, she changed the 'him' to 'her'. It was to remind me of my stubbornness. Sometimes with an eye roll, but often with relish. Her spoken delivery was so exact that I could see the horse, harnessed and saddled, the bit pulling at the lips and the foam gathering around the side of the mouth. The neck refusing to bow. The broken horse (and my goodness, I can remember the shock of understanding 'to break a horse') for a moment resisting the puny man and his whip. We all know that you cannot really break a horse. One swift kick of a hind leg, and it's very clear who has superior power. Charles again, and his concept of strength being only physical.

Nanna also used the expression about herself. This was accompanied by the glimmer of a smirk. But she never said it about her daughter, my compliant mother. We both knew that after a flash of resistance, Mother would drink the water, although she would have preferred wine.

The most humbling and humiliating realization a teacher has to make is that the student has to be *willing* to learn and work. However much you know, however well you explain the work, entertain, aim to please, no one learns deeply without being willing. This is particularly true of work that has to be embodied and demands presence, and therefore revelation.

Freeing the voice, freeing your energy and freeing the story is a difficult process. And whoever thinks educating and transforming is easy has never taught well. To lead others or yourself 'forth' is uncomfortable. The Reverend from the library introduced me to the Gospel of St Thomas. Jesus says, 'If you bring forth what is within you, what you will bring forth will save you. If you do not bring forth what is within you, what you do not bring forth will destroy you.' Yes, this I know now is the truth about myself and those I try to teach. And what is within us are sometimes shameful secrets that we keep from ourselves and the world. The secrets of not being or having enough of anything. Not enough intelligence, beauty, power. Not loved or liked enough. Not interesting or talented enough . . .

A student's willingness is out of my control, and therefore much of what I can do is redundant until they are willing to work, try and fail, and try again. One unwilling student can destroy the work of the whole group. Sometimes it is overt, but at other times there is a disguise of willingness that can mask laziness, carelessness or defiance. True willingness is an act of choice – of consent and openness.

Some of the conversations I heard in my early teaching among staff about unwilling students were brutal. 'You have to break them and then build them up.' Like horses? And what is left of their creativity, talent, uniqueness, after they are broken?

In corporate training, this is termed Command and Control, and is shorthand for an elite, patriarchal form of leadership.

A creative teacher has to be willing to teach in any way that draws forth the student's willingness and readiness to work. If the teacher is willing to teach and the student and group willing to learn, then anything is possible. The room transforms as natural presence and voice is rediscovered. Everyone is powerful, beautiful, talented, extraordinary. Willingness enables all divisions to dissolve, and then with willingly exercised work, we meet in our sameness and differences.

Women, we can join the table, sit down and be in our power with the best of men. We can stay present, and listen and speak, and not be interrupted or ignored – but we have to be willing to work and to lead well. Good leadership is clean and pure, not hidden or masked, but authentic and transparent. There are no games. Another of Nanna's sayings: *Cleanliness is close to godliness*.

In cleanliness, Nanna and Mother agreed. Both had a sense of pride in being clean and ordered. This is more remarkable when I imagine them in their Silver Place flat, with one bathroom serving the whole building. Both were constantly cleaning. Later in life, once we had moved out of London, my mother was often shocked when returning from being entertained at my father's wealthy friends' houses. These houses were not up to her level of cleanliness, and worse, neither were the hosts. She would remark upon expensive but dirty clothes, and fingers festooned with exquisite rings but with dirty fingernails. Even worse, these people smelled unwashed. One of Mother's explanations about why she first went out with my father was that, 'He smelled of soap.' She and Nanna would watch the hard-hitting television documentaries of the 1960s together, and join in speaking to the women on the screen: '*Wash the baby's face.*'

In voice work, I often find myself using cleaning images. When all the physical impediments are removed from body, breath and voice, a spring cleaning has to take place. The dust, cobwebs and sometimes rust, have to be scrubbed out of the instrument, in order to prepare for the voice's full power. Your voice has to be ready and willing to speak what matters to you.

Sin, morality and dirt were all the same to Nanna. 'Dirty unfair trick,' she would say. 'Filthy wrong idea,' 'Stinking bastard,' 'Stained woman.'

It seems obvious now that as I read *Hamlet* I would pick up and fuse together Shakespeare's images with hers. Bad leadership and any misuse of power was 'rotten', and that rottenness became part of the system. A rotten leader makes the State rotten. Within a few weeks after the death of a good king, *Something is rotten in the state of Denmark*. Nanna agreed. Hamlet feels this even before his father's ghost tells him the truth. His world is unclean, *an un-weeded garden, rank and gross*. 'It is not, nor it cannot come to good. But break my heart, for I must hold my tongue.'

The physical violence of holding your tongue results in the breaking of your heart. Not speaking out will damage you, break all you feel about yourself. By being silenced, we become diseased. Once I spotted these images of filth around bad leadership, I found them everywhere. Claudius, Hamlet's uncle, bought to consciousness of his crimes, says, 'What if this cursed hand were thicker than itself with brother's blood? Is there not rain enough in the sweet heavens to wash it white as snow?'

Macbeth, after killing Duncan, is covered in blood. Lady Macbeth believes the deed can be washed off – 'Go get some water and wash this filthy witness from your hand.' Macbeth knows otherwise: 'Will all great Neptune's oceans wash this blood clean from my hand? No this my hand will rather the multitudinous seas incarnadine, making the green one red.' He knows that even the sea cannot clean him. Lady Macbeth will only discover the truth in a sleepwalking nightmare as she tries to wash the blood off her hands: 'Out damned spot, out I say. What, will these hands ne're be clean. Here's the smell of the blood still. All the perfumes of Arabia will not sweeten this little hand.'

Shakespeare clearly teaches us that bad leadership is polluted and pollutes, and that good leadership cleans and renews. I began to notice that I was explaining that the main purpose in teaching leadership was to make it 'clean and transparent'. I had never learned corporate speak, so these uncomplicated words needed explaining and then to be embodied. Simply, there is no hidden agenda in good leadership. Equal and fair actions must be given to all the people that you lead. Clean justice, no favourites, no in-jokes, no gossip, no flirting. Nothing that allows a professional space to become non-inclusive.

A transparent leader works for no division but unity, and, crucially, a leader should not tolerate or encourage the keeping or defending of secrets. The greatest weapon in bad leadership is the keeping of secrets. Secrets destroy countries, companies and families. They allow bullies to thrive, sexual predators to flourish, cruelty to reign and intimidation to be normalized. Even when a secret is held for good reason, there will be a time when it begins to fester – and that is when a good leader cleans the wound by revelation.

The only people who fear revelation are those who protect themselves and a small 'club' around them with the secret. Those who control their clubs with secrets, actively keeping power and privilege to themselves – these are the clubs that have barred women for centuries. Every woman has encountered an exclusive club, figurative or real, that blocks their entrance. Some women manage to slip into these elite groups, but compromise their morality and reputation by becoming an efficiently supporting handmaiden to the club. This can include them receiving high office, and being well rewarded. But their price for inclusion is that they must exclude other women and threatening men. They will be required to defend incompetence and mediocrity, to keep the members of the club safe and their secrets buried.

It is the women, those outside power, who in Shakespeare risk witnessing a truth, a secret known in the club but never spoken. The speaking releases the speaker, and has the possibility of healing a country and the innocent victims in the country.

I wonder if Nanna would roll her eyes at my naiveté in believing that truth can set you free. It has, when I have spoken truth in the past, and I have never taught a woman who hasn't been relieved when the truth spills out of her mouth.

I believe what I think all storytellers believe – that when you speak out, it releases you, but also that your words, when fully spoken, enter and change others.

Words spoken exist long after the speaking.

Once spoken, you cannot unspeak them. Once heard, they cannot be unheard. It's gone on for too long, the violence and oppression.

The women in power must speak out with their full voice and presence, but also with fairness, decency and generosity towards the men who want to help. We know how harsh the misuse of power has been, and it has taken a toll on all women. We mustn't punish them as they have punished us, but choose a higher road. The mess of brutal, male power has destroyed too much, and taken, without giving back, from women and the planet.

Enough is enough.

Nanna, a working-class woman born in 1886, had no choice but to bow to her 'betters'. But, although she was hobbled by circumstance, she was always secure in the certainty that they weren't better than her. She never felt the need to make anyone who had power over her feel comfortable. Her own display of power was to refuse to beg to be heard, or to try to please, but to stay secure in her own righteous knowledge. She would have joined a band of witches on the heath, or the Furies, if she had encountered them. Her choices were further limited because, although striking – she was often called a handsome woman – she wasn't considered a beauty like my petite mother.

Margaret, my mother, didn't have choices either, and blamelessly chose to be kept safe but neglected, in her beautiful cage in the suburbs.

Women of my generation, believing we had been given equality, burst through the door that had been barred to us for millennia, expecting to be welcomed and invited to sit at the table of power by the men around us. When that didn't happen, we tried to appease them, tried to be them, raged and pushed . . . and when none of this worked, some chose to withdraw again, and keep their head below the parapet. To stay still and silent to maintain their dignity.

But, I see so much hope in the sure-footed young women who are honouring each other and the planet, who are finding ways to speak their full power and equality. Who are, with their natural, centred Second Circle power, unstoppable: they are changing the world.

I feel privileged to live in this moment, when young women are balanced enough to know that they must not misuse their power, but that they must use it. All over the world, women are realizing that their knowledge and their stories are crucial.

Against all the odds, more and more are stepping forward, finding the sweet spot at the centre of the see-saw, standing earthed, and taking the deep, clean breath that will release their woman's voice.

INDEX